Behavioral Interview

Pass More Easily a Behavioral Interview Because You Are Totally Relaxed. Relax Your Mind and Learn to Believe in Yourself.

Horatio Bird

Table of Content

Introduction

Chapter 1: Introduction to Behavioral Interview

Importance of Behavioral Interview Technique to Employers

Provide an Opportunity to Demonstrate Real-Life Experience

Behavioral Questions are Easily Customized

Provides Better Intuition in Hiring Decision Making

It Enables Prospective Candidates to be More Comfortable

Preparing for The Behavioral Interview

Know the Competencies of the Employer

Come Up with Work-Related Examples

Make Use of Group Projects

Write Your Stories in Detail

How to Be Relaxed and Confident During the Behavioral Interview

Connect with the Interviewer

Use Breathing Techniques to Boost Your Confidence

Don't Judge Yourself Harshly

Picture Yourself Succeeding

Prepare by Rehearsing Your Answers Aloud

Difficulties Associated with Passing Behavioral Interviews as Highlighted in Recent Researches

Not Each Great Candidate Has an Answer

Candidates Need a Lot of Time to Think Back

Focuses Too Much on the Negative

Hard to Answer Challenging Questions

Chapter 2: The Essentials of a Star Behavioral Interview

What Makes A Behavioral Interview Valid?

Situation

Task

Action

Result

Common Behavioral Interview Questions

Steps on How to Prepare for Behavioral Questions Using The STAR

Chapter 3: Preparing for The Behavioral Interview

Study of Job Description

Review Your Past Projects

Revisit Previous Job Performance Reviews

List Down Your Professional Accomplishments

Need for Honesty and Openness in Interview Answers

Keeping Your Answers Short

Chapter 4: Behavioral Interview Questions

Common Questions

Problem-Solving, Creativity, Initiative

How to Handle Questions on Problem-Solving?

How to Handle Questions on Teamwork?

How to Handle Questions on Organizational Skills?

How to Handle Questions on Adaptability?

How to Handle Negotiation Questions?

How to Handle Questions About Work Ethic?

Chapter 5: Sample Thank-You Letters

The Intricate Interview Process

General Thank-You Letter Outline

Sample Letter 1: Formal Business Thank-You Letter

Sample Letter 2: Small to Medium Enterprise Thank-You Letter

Sample Letter 3: Start-Ups

Points to Note:

Chapter 6: Expectancy of Employers and Their Tactics

Tips to Conduct an Effective Behavioral Interview

Characteristics and Traits Expected by The Employer During A Behavioral Interview

Chapter 7: Your Curriculum Vitae

The Relevance of a Curriculum Vitae

Components of A Quality CV

Chapter 8: The Team Spirit

What the Interviewer Wants to Know

How to Respond: "State Instances of Your Teamwork"

Chapter 9: Dealing with Rejection after a Behavioral Job Interview

How to Deal with Rejection After A Behavioral Job Interview

Remember it is Not All About You

Rejection is Never Feedback.

Don't Carry Interview Baggage Around with You

Keep Learning and Developing

Learn to Stay Positive

Stay Connected by Sending a Thank You Letter

Appreciate Your Effort

Ask Your Interviewer to Consider You for Future Openings

Analyze Your Resume

Hire a Career Coach

Be Flexible to the Needs of Your Next Job Search

- Take Up an Extra Project at Work to Build Your Experience and Resume
- Try Again Applying for a Vacancy at Your Dream Company
- Apply for as Many Job Openings as Possible
- Allow Yourself Time to Grieve
- Take a Walk

The Reasons for The Job Rejection
- Failure to Keep Time
- Failure to Follow Instructions
- You Were Unpolished
- They Think You Won't Stay for Long with Them
- Awkward Nonverbal Cues

Bonus Chapter: Tips on How to Pass the Behavioral Interview

- Prepare Well for Common Behavioral Interview Questions
- Guidelines to Structure A Behavioral Interview
  - Include Enough Details in Your Answer
  - Listen Carefully to Each Question Asked
  - Use Recent Examples in Your Answer
  - Handle Negative Situations Confidently
  - Vary Your Examples
  - Stick to the Facts
  - Be Aware of Your Body Language

Practice Your Answers

Come Up With a List of Competencies, Attributes, and Skills

Create a List of Your Experience

Focus on the Good and the Bad

Make Use of the STAR Method

Take a Look at Your Past Performance Documents and Appraisals

Start Your Preparation Now

What Does the Interviewer Want in Behavioral Interview Answers?

Common Mistakes to Avoid Doing Behavioral Interviews

Failing to Prepare

Failing to Research Your Interviewer

Putting on the Wrong Outfit

Not Being Punctual

Using Your Cellphone During the Interview

Asking Questions with Obvious Answers

Talking Bad About Past Employers

Getting Too Personal

Asking for Salary and Benefits Details Too Soon

Failure to Anticipate Questions About Salary

Having Poor Body Language

Lying

Failing to Sell Your Skills

Selling Yourself Too Aggressively

Neglecting to Ask Questions

Faking the Answers to Questions About Your Most Significant Weaknesses

Conclusion

Introduction

Congratulations on buying *Behavioral Interview: Pass More Easily A Behavioral Interview Because You Are Totally Relaxed. Relax Your Mind and Learn to Believe in Yourself,* and thank you for doing so. Most people attend several behavioral interviews, but end up failing due to the lack of understanding of the basic requirements. By reading this book, you have taken the first step towards learning how to prepare yourself for a behavioral interview. The information that you find in the following chapters is very important as it will help you to know the dos and don'ts of such an interview and the way to react to an interview rejection.

The purpose of this book is to guide you and demonstrate to you on how to effectively pass a behavioral interview when being hired. By using the techniques presented, you will be able to get absorbed in most of the interviews you engage in. Is it worth it? You bet! Research has indicated that most employers are looking for good workers who are able to contribute up to 70% equivalence of their monetary value (salary paid). Better interviewing processes are also associated with reduced emotional and monetary costs incurred when hiring. A behavioral interview is also associated with reduced material damage, reduced customer complaints, null replacement hiring, and reduced accidents.

To that end, this book covers the basic concepts of a behavioral interview. Also, it incorporates key interviewing elements that can help you pass a behavioral interview, including the essentials of a STAR behavioral interview, how to prepare for this type of interview, the common behavioral interview questions that employers ask, sample thank you letters that are relevant after you win a job, and how to handle any interview rejections. All these elements are essential to increase your validity and effectiveness in responding to a behavioral interview. Through this guide, you will be able to approach the interview in a relaxed manner with a lot of confidence.

Chapter 1: Introduction to Behavioral Interview

When you are invited for a job interview, chances are you will participate in a behavioral interview. Unlike the regular job interviews, behavioral interviews are conducted by employers to find out whether you have done a particular task in the past rather than if you can do it. The hiring manager will expect you to demonstrate your competencies in a given area by giving specific examples from your experience at work, school, and in life. And from the experience you present, the interviewers will determine whether you possess the necessary knowledge, skills, and abilities to perform a task they are interviewing you for.

The hiring manager will also determine the specific competencies required to perform a particular job for which you applied and then come up with several behavioral questions that will enable them to know whether you have the desired competencies or not.

Many of these behavioral questions dwell on your soft skills. These are the skills that will enable you to effectively perform your duties, including solving problems that may arise in the course of your task. Other areas of interest to your interviewer may include your critical thinking, listening, interpersonal, and speaking skills.

The basic premise of the behavioral interview is that your past performance is an excellent predictor of how you will perform in the future. This may be the reason why many candidates feel intimidated by the behavioral interview technique. However, you should not, behavioral interview offers you a fantastic opportunity to showcase to your prospective employer that you are the right candidate for a particular job.

A regular job interview will only limit you to telling your interviewer what you are capable of. Still, in a behavioral interview, you get an opportunity to describe in detail how you handled a particular situation in real life. You tell your interviewer, "I have done it before, and I will do it again when an opportunity arises."

The format of behavioral interview questions is mostly rigid and predictable. Most interview questions start with "can you tell me about a specific time when..." or "can you give me a detailed example or when...." however, there are no standard answers for the behavioral interview questions. If you don't have experience in a given area then it is hard to make up an answer.

Importance of Behavioral Interview Technique to Employers

Most regular job interview requires you to reply to simple yes or no questions. A candidate, therefore, can quickly tell the interviewer what they need to hear. However, behavioral interviews demand that you give a real-life example, which has details of how you handled a particular situation. An interviewer can also ask several follow up questions to confirm whether you really dealt with the situation or not. It is, therefore, essential for you to always give candid and honest answers rather than making up a story. If you lack any experience to relate with, it is advisable to provide a hypothetical situation. Other benefits of behavioral interviews include the following:

Provide an Opportunity to Demonstrate Real-Life Experience

Behavioral interview questions offer you a chance to walk the talk. You can quickly write in your CV that you have excellent leadership skills, or you are a good problem solver. If you were not honest in what you stated in your CV, then your potential employer will quickly unmask you by the use of behavioral questions. A study recently conducted revealed that 85 percent of applicants falsely alter their resumes and applications. Behavioral questions help a lot in solving this challenge by forcing the candidates to go beyond their resumes.

It is quite challenging to make up solid examples of experience in an interview room as compared to merely stating a falsity in a resume.

Behavioral Questions are Easily Customized

Traditional interview questions can be easily predicted. All you need is simple preparation to correctly answer usual questions such as "what are your strengths and weaknesses." Behavioral questions, on the other hand, can be tailor-made to fit the employment opportunity at hand. The behavioral interview questions will, therefore, be unique to that particular interview. Because of this, it is a challenge for you to prepare for them or to come up with false answers. Your interviewer will quickly see through your well-polished and rehearsed answers.

Provides Better Intuition in Hiring Decision Making

One of the most critical factors for being able to work well in a particular workplace is your ability to perform well within a given structure of the organization's culture. At times you may possess exceptional skills and experience, but you will fail to match them to the demands of a specific job. Behavioral interviews allow the interviewers to get an understanding of your personality and what motivates and drives you. If you are a good team player and have an excellent experience, but you lack a high level of autonomy, which is a crucial requirement for the position you are applying, then you are not the right person for that particular job. The only way the interviewer can get this kind of information from you is by employing the behavioral questions during the interview sessions.

It Enables Prospective Candidates to be More Comfortable

Often the most qualified candidates are the worst interviewees. When their nerves are pricked, the most suitable candidates end up projecting themselves in a negative light. With behavioral interviews, the candidates are made more comfortable and less nervous because the questions tend to flow naturally, and the conversation is quite friendly and enjoyable. The experience of behavioral interviews is the same as being asked to narrate a story in a normal conversation, you will, therefore, feel more comfortable, and you get rid of feelings of anxiety or nervousness.

Preparing for The Behavioral Interview

You might experience challenges on how to prepare for a behavioral interview. You, therefore, need to prepare well in the following areas:

Know the Competencies of the Employer

You should always seek to know the specific competencies the employer is seeking. You, therefore, need to go through the job description thoroughly. If you are working with a recruiter, you can book an appointment and talk with them, but remember not to canvass. Do thorough research on the company to familiarize yourself with its working and their expectations. The following are some of the common competencies which most behavioral interviewers look at:

- Level of enthusiasm
- Team building
- Conflict resolution
- Technical skills specific for the job
- Problem-solving skills
- Leadership qualities
- Interpersonal skills
- Decision-making skills
- Listening skills
- Verbal communication skills

After determining the specific competencies, you need to come up with relevant examples of how to demonstrate those competencies in past situations. You can list down all the questions you expect your interviewer to ask and recall your experiences in the previous jobs in which you have had to use those competencies.

Come Up with Work-Related Examples

You should always come up with work-related answers to behavioral questions asked by your interviewer. However, if you can't find any experience to relate with, then it is okay to pick examples from your time in school. However, your work experience may be limited if you are a recent graduate.

Make Use of Group Projects

You should revert to group projects for excellent opportunities that will enable you to demonstrate the skills required by your employer. Such projects can include the time you spent participating in sports with your colleagues.

Write Your Stories in Detail

You need to write down your relevant stories and examples in as much detail as possible. Give specific information about what happened, who was involved, and what exactly did you do to arrive at the desired outcome. You also need to come up with both positive and negative examples. Your interviewer will most likely seek to know about the particular situations you were not able to favorably solve an issue and the lessons you picked from that specific failure.

How to Be Relaxed and Confident During the Behavioral Interview

Connect with the Interviewer
During your interview, you should strive to create a likable impression with your interviewer. You should, therefore, build your confidence by creating a positive rapport with your interviewer from the word go. However, you should not attempt to impress your hiring manager. Confidence is more about putting yourself at ease by connecting with others rather than your performance.

Use Breathing Techniques to Boost Your Confidence
Breathing and mindfulness will significantly help you build up your confidence levels. When you focus on your breath, you stay alert and present to your current

decisions, which will help calm down your nerves, especially before an interview. Whenever you are anxious, your blood will flow away from your brain because you are on a flight or fight mode, and they will hamper your cognitive functions. You, therefore, need to calm down by taking three deep breaths whenever you sense anxiety creeping in.

Don't Judge Yourself Harshly

You need to speak to yourself with a lot of compassion before the interview. Get rid of all the critical thoughts that may stand in your way. Tell yourself you are great and can perform the interview well. You should also not be afraid to sell your skills before the interview panel.

Picture Yourself Succeeding

You need to boost your confidence by picturing yourself succeeding in your interview. Visualize a successful interview scenario, imagine yourself walking into the interview room, shaking your interviewer's hands, and answering their questions confidently. When you strongly believe that you are the right person for that particular job and you relax into that confidence, then it will significantly help.

Prepare by Rehearsing Your Answers Aloud

When you approach an interview with well-researched answers to every possible question, then you faceless anxiety, and your confidence level will be on the rise. When you think you know the answers to every question they will ask, you tend to be more confident. You can rehearse potential interview questions with a friend. Such rehearsal will help you to be well prepared for the interview. You will also get an opportunity to deal with any weak areas whenever you rehearse before an interview. Focus on specific skills, experience, and knowledge as well as your personal qualities and examples which you think are relevant to the particular job you are being interviewed for.

Difficulties Associated with Passing Behavioral Interviews as Highlighted in Recent Researches

Behavioral interview questions are much tougher than traditional interview questions. Because they require specific answers, you experience challenges preparing for them. They also seek to expose a lot about your personality, character, as well as your abilities. Although every recruiter is nowadays embracing this interview technique, there are several glaring weaknesses associated with behavioral interviews, which were revealed in recent studies. These difficulties may include:

Not Each Great Candidate Has an Answer

Some of the behavioral interview questions may require you to come up with an answer which you don't genuinely have. You may be presented with a question whose answers you can't relate with. It will be unfair for the interview to judge your performance based on how you answer such questions.

Candidates Need a Lot of Time to Think Back

You may need a lot of time to think back to particular experiences when answering behavioral questions. This will not only make the whole interview experience awkward but will result in time wastage. Some questions require specific answers, and you will not always have a ready answer on your fingertips.

Focuses Too Much on the Negative
A study reveals that the most useful behavioral interview questions often focus on the negatives. Such negativity can affect the whole interview process, how you view the company and your expectations of the job you are being interviewed for.

Hard to Answer Challenging Questions
You are more likely to make mistakes answering hard questions. Some great applicants may not necessarily oases the right talent on how to tackle hard issues, although they may have the right skills and knowledge for the job they are being interviewed for. Generally, behavioral questions are hard, and the harder they are, the more likely for good workers to make mistakes when answering them.

Chapter 2: The Essentials of a Star Behavioral Interview

Behavioral job interviews are currently considered by so many companies. The interview questions will want a persuasive illustration of your skills and experiences that are concerning the position you wish to, unlike the traditional job interview questions that will only ask you to talk about what you did in character or to share your experiences. You should be able to note that questions will be generally formatted by bringing forth a situation inquiring about what step you have taken to respond to something similar previously and what was the result.

The interviewer will ask you how you will handle a situation, and you will have to answer with a clarification of what you did. The main idea of this is to show your success previously has some positive impact on your success forthcoming. You possibly don't need to have answers in memorized in your mind, or have a sense of your experiences that you would want to share and tell about them to the interviewer.

1. **Describe to the interviewer how you have been working effectively under pressure**
    The interviewer considering giving you a highly stressful job, they will want to know how good you are working under pressure. You should be able to bring out real examples that show your

previous experiences with stress and how you handled the situation.

2. **How you handle challenges and an example**

Despite your job, there may be issues, and it may not turn out to be business as usual. When such questions come up, the person doing the interview will want you to tell them how you will react when you experience such awkward moments. You should have a focus on how you solved a thought-provoking condition when you respond.

3. **Do you ever make mistakes, and how do you handle them?**

There is no one perfect, and all of us will make a mistake or two at some point. The hiring manager will want to know how you took the situation when you made a mistake.

4. **Describe how you set your objectives**

The interviewer is much interested in how you come up with your plans and set the goals that you will want to execute. You can quickly get through this by giving out examples that you have experienced or have seen about successful goal setting.

5. **Talk about the goals that you have accomplished and how you did it**
The interviewer will have an interest in getting to know what you do for you to achieve your goals and which steps do you take for you to execute them.

6. **Instances of how you worked on a team**
A lot of jobs will want you to work as part of a team. An interviewer or the hiring manager will want to know how well to carry yourself when with others and how you cooperate with the other team members around you and the people you work with.

What Makes A Behavioral Interview Valid?

The most known interview queries that you will always come through are the behavioral questions.

You will always come through such kinds of questions anytime you get into an interview despite what type of industry you discuss with. You should be able to know how you handle them and know what they entail. Here are some of the things that can assist you to go through. There are some elements of a STAR concept, as discussed below.

Situation
This, as the first component, will want you to know about the context of your response. You are supposed to use this component as the primary basis to expound details of the kinds of situations that you want to talk more about.

Task
This your second component in the STAR method, and it will involve the impact that you had in that environment. This component will not want to look at what you did, but it wants to look at what is expected in this situation.

Action

You have to move on to the next step by describing the activities you have by beginning to solve the situation. This component will put its focus on specific actions and the reasons why you took the actions. It is all about what happened in the real sense and not what should have been happening.

Result

This is the last component of the STAR method, and it will want to know the outcome of the aspect of everything generally. It will put all its focus on the finer details of the issue and try to understand the actions in the past components that brought about this particular outcome.

Common Behavioral Interview Questions

In cases where you have a group of individuals working towards a specific mission common amongst them in your workplace, as an employer, you will want to know how the employees will react to various circumstances. As a good employee, it is not all about being gifted to perform a role technically, but you should also be able to handle the situations that will come along with the task. Below are some of the common behavioral questions:

- You will have to talk about times when you worked closely with an individual whose personality was different from yours.
- You will be expected to talk about a situation that you wish to have handled differently with your colleague.
- You are supposed to give an example on times when you didn't meet your clients' anticipation. What happened, and what was your attempt to correct the situation?
- What are your priorities?
- Can you be able to talk about the times that you failed or succeeded? How was your reaction to the situation?
- What was your greatest achievement?
- What are the ways that help you to motivate yourself?
- Have you been able to face any conflict, what did you do?

- Are you able to give an example of a time that you tried to persuade someone?
- How do you go about your responsibilities?

Behavioral questions that you are asked will bring about some core things like:

- Ways that you can handle certain situations
- Your thinking capabilities
- Your comparison with other candidates

Such elements will give room for the interviewer to understand you deeply as a candidate. The questions will move deeper into your personality and talent that you will bring along to the workplace and what technical abilities you have to perform the role you have been given. The hiring manager will want to know about some of the things about your character when they ask you about behavioral questions. At first, they will want to see how you used to behave previously in real-world occasions. This will be very vital because the questions are not all about imagination situations, the hiring manager doesn't want to know how they will behave, but all they want to know is how you behaved.

Secondly, the questions want to know and understand the values that you have been able to add to the real situation. The person conducting the interview will want to see what you did and what are some of the expectations that made you influence the outcome. This is not all about what someone did, a group or organization did, or something that someone else presents there did, it wants to know your actions and characters and how they have an impact on the situation. The hiring manager will want to know about your activities and styles and what are the activities that you took to impress the condition.

Finally, the hiring manager will want to know how you will define and analyze various workplace conditions. This will give them a platform to have a comparison between you and the other candidates and assist them in analyzing your capability that fits to work environment. This means you should be able to define things like success, failure, and mistake. A hiring manager is not looking for you to tell them about the real steps and the actions that you settled on. The interests they have are seeing the kind of situation you will describe to be a trial. Many people will consider unique workplace circumstances as a trial.

Steps on How to Prepare for Behavioral Questions Using The STAR

There are ways that you can begin using STAR, and it will be to your advantage, and you can get its grasp by:

- Knowing the concept of the STAR
- Reasons why you are being asked behavioral queries
- Ways in which STAR will assist you to respond to the queries

Some easy steps will help you to prepare for behavioral questions with STAR

1. **Have a list of your skills and experiences**
   You should begin by first having a list of your skills and experiences. These will help you to have a good and essential performance and the role that you have succeeded after applying for it. It is not just about listing skills and the

qualifications that you have, and this is because you have a lot of them. The main thing is for you to have focus on the core skills that you want for a specific particular role. For you to find out what they are, then you have to look at the job listing. You have to able to read it, underline any skill and experiences that have been mentioned by the employer and note them down in a chart. You can list many or few as they are wanted. The main point is to get the core skills behaviors that will assist you in the role and detailed task environment. You can also put into consideration other skills that the employer has not mentioned, but you know they can be of help. They can be closely related to the skills the employer said and what you have.

2. Choose a situation where you showcased the ability or experience

For now, you have the skills listed down. By this time, you are aware of what the employer wants and the skills your answers should have an impact on, and you have to show the skills in action. The next move you are making is about matching every talent with an actual life example. You have to get the SITUATION in STAR. You are encouraged to choose on what you have done, dealt with at some point, and you have been able to accomplish. You have to give context to your skills and appearances. It can be better when you provide examples of the situation the same as the one that you want to deal with in the new role.

3. **Note down the STAR functions**

At this point, you have to bring out your STAR template and read through every example and giving them a STAR treatment. Some templates can assist you in filling vital points that you come along. The questions in the models can be a guide when you want to write an answer. When you get to this point, then you can inscribe something close to an oral answer that you can give. You are allowed to have sample questions that are common behavioral queries with your responses. What you have to know is how to highlight your skills and use actual examples as your responses, and you have to master the STAR strategy.

There are a few examples of behavioral job interview questions and STAR answers. For you to have the best experience, then you have to get some ideas on how to look at some examples. Some core behavioral queries are mostly unanimously asked when in job interviews. You can get to know about instances of answers or responses to the questions that have been highlighted by the STAR strategy. You are supposed to talk about the time that you were a leader and what you did. Have you ever been in a position to make a mistake? How were you able to work on it? Tell the hiring manager about an example of a goal that you have executed and how you were able to make it successful.

When you can use the STAR strategy, then you will be able to be the star of the job interview that you have gone through. Behavioral queries will assist you because they are a very vital part of the job interview. They will be used to asses you very carefully, and you will be able to analyze your fit in the company. They can tell the hiring manager who you are and the things that you have done to make some predictions about your experience in the role. When you want to answer the questions, then the best method to use will be the STAR technique. It will assist in highlighting the right elements of your past performance and will give your responses the right kind of structure and level of a feature.

The best way for you to respond to behavioral questions is by using the STAR technique. This can be a structured way you will be forming an answer. STAR also stands for Situation, Task, Action, Result. STAR matrix is a strange way that you can use for you to prepare for interviews and how you can make it possible for it to be downloaded as part of this tutorial. When you want to be successful with the behavioral-based interview, then you have to prepare well. What will kill the features of the

STAR matrix is that it will force you to think more about your experiences. When you complete the matrix, then you put the skills in your short-term memory. When you come across the behavioral-based questions, then you will have an answer ready for the interviewer.

Some suggestions can help you use the STAR matrix as follows:

1. **Situations**

    It can be your first job, and you don't have to worry because everyone else as somewhere to begin with. The conditions that you have should not draw anything upon your career. In cases where you are to choose a situation, then you will have to use a variety when it's possible. When you are still new in the career, then you can likely involve a combination of stories from your job, school experience, and freestyle tasks.

2. **Tasks**

   You should keep your chores short and sweet. Generally, you will have to know it's your role in the situation and how the character started to be your problem or the position, to begin with.

3. **Actions**

   These are the steps that you ought to take in a situation. Your potential employer will have their focus on how you handle stressful cases that you come across. What are the steps that you have taken to solve it? There are some traits that employers will use in judging potential employees:

   - **Initiative** – How will potential employees find out that there is a problem to start with?
   - **Approach** – What is the plan you have in solving a problem? Are you able to make decisions on how to handle things immediately, or you have to gather

opinions and information on how to move on?
- **Goal-Setting** – When you begin taking actions, are you thinking what the outcome will look like?

When you are talking about your actions, be sure about putting your best foot ahead. You should have in mind what you want; someone will feel like working with you or for you.

4. **Results**

These are a very vital part of the STAR framework. You can decide to frame the perfect situation and try to describe how smooth your actions are, and it will matter if a won't focus on the outcomes. You should be able to frame the results that you had gained against the situation when you started. Some tips assist in conveying your achievements during an interview.

- You can put your results in terms of financial impact in cases where you are in a revenue-driving part of a business-

like sales. You should concentrate on income created, businesses that have been won, and the future value of the clients that you added.
- Concentrate on the time savings that will have an impact on the team in cases where you have implemented a new report or analysis.

You should always have in mind that your main objective is to show a track record of success for the hiring manager to give you the job. You should link the previous achievements to the questions that you are having at hand. In mind, you should remember that having success in an interview is not the luck of the draw. When you are willing to follow all the steps of finishing the STAR matrix and have a review of your responses, then you will possibly be successful in behavioral interview occasions. There are some significant takeaways when you want to prepare for a behavioral interview, such as:

- A lot of companies tend to use a behavioral interview to assist them in getting to know how employees with capability will be able to handle conditions.
- When you follow the STAR framework on occasions when you are answering queries will assist in having your responses concise and frame how you will be able to work on situations.
- You should know that it is essential to finish the STAR matrix for you to place your matrix responses in short term memory and craft the narrative that your forthcoming boss should be able to know.

Some tutorials can help you to prepare for an interview when you read or go through them. They are as follows:

- You should look at the tutorials and business instructors on the web that has excellent tutorials on how you can be able to respond to

complicated behavioral queries. You have the option of putting them in the STAR matrix, and you will see it out for them.
- There is also a good journal on how you can respond to the most common twenty interview queries.

Chapter 3: Preparing for The Behavioral Interview

Many employers would wish to pick the best candidates during interviews for the jobs they offer. For this reason, apart from using the traditional interviewing way of asking hypothetical questions, they use the behavioral type of interview whereby they ask situational questions. It is a way in which they have the best chance to have knowledge about your past behavior and probably how you are going to behave in the future. It is, therefore, important for you to prepare yourself for the behavioral interview, to ensure that you have the answers to the possible questions to be asked during the interview.

Interviewers will want to know how you overcome real difficult situations at work. For example, they may ask you to mention one challenging problem you may have come across in your last job and how you solved it. It will help them to know how you react to such problems, and if you add any measurable value in handling the problems. Preparing for the behavioral interview goes beyond the interview and has its benefits. For examples, stories you come up with may help you at networking, you will equip yourself properly when you prepare for a behavioral-based interview, it will help you have a good record of your past accomplishments to use for bios, and it will assist in building your confidence.

In this regard, we are going to look into the preparation checklist of a behavioral interview that can help you plan well for the interview, and help you to maneuver this uphill challenge. It is never easy, but preparing properly will make things easier.

Study of Job Description

My hunch is that you have been invited for a job interview before. Therefore, I am sure you are familiar with the feeling it comes with receiving that email; Much excitement. And, of course, it doesn't last long before that distinct feeling of being thrown into a den of lions that follows almost immediately. However, no need for panic, there is a secret weapon many people do not realize their importance, and that is a job description. With job description, there you have a powerful resource at your disposal that can help you pass that behavioral interview successfully.

While for most people, a job description is to detail you the position primarily, there is much more; it can help you prepare for the interview. With the job description, you can come up with mock interview questions you can practice. For example, from the job description, the position requires someone with the ability to work in a team. Therefore, it can help you create a behavioral interview question like "Tell me about a time you worked in a team." You need to go through the entire job description and try to turn everything into a question. Then, with these mock questions, you can practice to answer them aloud, either alone in a room or with the help of a friend you trust.

Additionally, when you are walking into a behavioral interview room, it would be smart and brilliant to have a few good stories with you. I can't imagine the best place to figure out the kind of stories that are most appropriate to share with the interviewers apart from the job description. Go through the skills the position calls for, and for each of the skills outlined, come up with an anecdote. For example, you can think of that time you showcased your project management skills, and you had to communicate to a non-technical audience; this is quite a skill, the ability to communicate to the audience that doesn't understand the technical part of the project, and make them understand.

Therefore, it is a good idea focus on the job description as it has a wealth of knowledge that can guide you as you prepare for that behavioral job interview.

Review Your Past Projects

Most positions that require some project management skills will have your interviewers asking a competency-based question. For instance, you can be asked to describe an important project you worked on before. There are reasons as to why interviewers will ask you this question. They want to have insight on how well you can manage a project, how the skills can aid you to lead a project, and the approach you used in overcoming challenges and situations when handling the project.

It will be hard for you to give a five-star answer to this kind of question if you haven't prepped well before the interview. You must prepare in advance the answers you will respond to such questions. First, you need to list all the important projects you have worked on before this interview. Note down the goals of each project, specifying your role in the project, and then the results of all the projects.

What is also important is that you choose the right example of the project you will tell to interviewers. Most interviewees realize halfway that they are narrating the wrong project, which can cause some damage to your interview. It is a brilliant idea to focus on the most recent project- it is because you don't want to give the impression that your last significant and important project you had in your career occurred eons ago. Moreover, you have to ensure you choose a successful project unless you want to share how you turned an unsuccessful project around and made it successful. It is also vital that you pick an example of a project, which aligns with the responsibilities and duties of the job for the job in question.

Additionally, if you were on a managing role in a project, it will not be enough just to highlight a few responsibilities when narrating the important achievement/project in your career. It is because the interviewer wants to know how you made the decisions you made or how you led your team. Not only what you have done. Also, you have to avoid the mistake of saying "we" all the time when responding to the questions about your important project. Explain clearly your specific contributions to the project and emphasize the roles you played in making it a success.

Revisit Previous Job Performance Reviews

If you are job hunting, I am sure you must have spent your time in polishing your resume and rehearsing Q's & A's of commonly asked questions in an interview. You may, however, have overlooked the most important tool that can sway the interviewers' decision in your favor, which is offering performance appraisals from your previous jobs. Appraisals are trusted by employers to give an honest look at how you performed in your previous jobs, which will give an added advantage if your last employer thought highly of you.

Therefore, if you are looking for a job, and the company you worked with previously did not conduct these reviews, you can let your previous boss know you are looking for a job and you would like him or her to write you a formal evaluation of your records at the company to raise your chances of landing a new job. Alternatively, you can write your assessment and ask them to review and make edits.

During the interview, you can share your past appraisals by responding to the questions from the interviewer about how you performed in your last job with the comments from your previous employer. For instance, if an interviewer asks about what you know or think is your greatest strength, you can respond to this by pointing out how your last review your employer praised your ability to show leadership in a team. You can also leave the copies of your reviews with the interviewer. Carry a copy of the appraisal in a file folder so that you hand it over to the interviewer at the end of the interview.

Moreover, one can use the reviews to demonstrate a history of performance improvement. For instance, if the previous review recommended an area to make some improvement, carry a later appraisal that shows you heeded the advice and made changes. Also, you choose to discuss how you learned from the experience and how you have worked to ensure you are a more effective employee. By sharing this information with your interviewer, high chances are it will work in your favor and get you your dream job. Therefore, as you prepare for a behavioral interview, you must take your time to revisit your previous job performance reviews.

List Down Your Professional Accomplishments

The interviewer is in the room because they want to find the best candidate for the job position, which fell vacant. It is most likely that an interviewer asks about your career accomplishments. It is not an easy question to ask, and I bet you agree; it is neither comfortable for most people to share their career achievements. For most people who are introvert, this can be challenging. Sharing or rather "bragging" their achievements can seem rude or obnoxious to them.

However, you must understand that what may look as rude or bragging at the cocktail party, is much welcomed and acceptable in a job interview. For an interviewer, it is impossible to understand a candidate enough or know how great they are just by going through their resume or a small chat. Asking this behavioral question is the most reliable way for him or her to get a sense of how the candidate goes about their work and who they are. Therefore, when asked this question, you do not want to throw it away through the window. It is a perfect opportunity for you to share with the interviewer the most impressive experience in your career. If you are not comfortable sharing about yourself and your accomplishments, then you are not doing yourself justice or any level of fairness by letting the best opportunities thrown at you slip away.

But also, you need to be careful as you do this not to look as someone full of oneself, rude, or entitled. You can dodge this situation by preparing in advance. When you prepare well, it will help you get comfortable to discuss yourself and your accomplishments positively and naturally that display confidence and proud but not arrogance or cockiness.

Therefore, as someone who truly wants to win that dream job interview, you have to make a list of all the achievements that you have accomplished in your career. When an interviewer asks you to tell the best achievement in your life, it will give you the power to choose the story you want to highlight. It also presents you with an opportunity for you to influence how the interviewer views you. Thus, you have to be well prepared for you to be in a position to choose an example properly you think it will sell your suitability for the job in the best manner possible. It is important not to end up choosing the underwhelming example, which doesn't emphasize your best contributions and thinking. The example you pick will help the interviewer envision you at your best work rate. Also, it will guide them to understand what you value most, which will inform them to know if you are the best fit for the job. I recommend that you prepare well and set 3-5 best stories if you sense the interview will be heavily behavioral-based and take your time in strategizing what examples you will highlight and how

Need for Honesty and Openness in Interview Answers

Employers will always wish to hire people who are honest, professional, and show openness. Recruiters want confident and down to earth employees, but they can only determine if you are a good fit for the company when you are honest and open. In regards to your skills, performance, experience, and qualifications, you must always be honest- otherwise, you are shooting yourself in the foot.

Honesty and openness are virtues, and they do matter a lot during interviews. Naturally, candidates want to appear as favorably as possible during a job interview. They want to look perfect, that they are walking in a thin line between boasting and honesty. You may not want to embellish your expertise and experiences. For example, you may write in your resume that you are highly fluent in the Japanese language, then be ready to demonstrate your skills in the interview, when requested. Remember, once you have gotten a job, your employer may hand you a huge project- for example handling a merger between a large Japanese corporation and your company. Oops. Having confidence in your talents and skills is a nice thing, but make sure that you remain open and honest; otherwise, things can get nasty one day.

When an interviewer asks you about the experience you have regarding leadership in the position in question, tell the interviewer where your leadership skills lie and back up your argument with concrete examples. You should always aim to indicate your level of leadership with openness and honesty. For example, there is a huge difference in leading a department or a team consisting of only five interns. Always be sincere since even leading the interns have given you some experience, and you can use the same knowledge and experience in the position in question. In this way, recruiters can get a clear image of who you are, and they will be aware right from the beginning if you need any further training, the kind of further developments which could be helpful to you, and the departments which you can best offer your knowledge.

Furthermore, when reacting to questions regarding your weaknesses and any missing areas of knowledge, you must react to them tactfully. In these situations, you must prepare. You can consider in advance how you will react to such questions. You don't have to choose weaknesses that seem only to disguise strengths. Rather, you need to pick the real weaknesses, show that you acknowledge, and how you are working to improve on them. For example, you can mention something like difficulty in addressing large crowd, and that you have attended seminars on public speaking for the last three months in trying to resolve the problem.

Keeping Your Answers Short

Some people have some specialty when it comes to rambling. Perhaps silence is not their thing, and they find themselves letting all their thoughts pour down. However, this habit is not productive in all scenarios, especially not in an interviewing room. Therefore, if you are that type of person, I suggest that you work on it because it can be a deal-breaker. This rambling person will eventually come to answer the question, but only after sharing too many backgrounds in painstaking detail. He or she does not realize the importance of giving just the right amount of information at the right moment. It is not really brief just for the sake, but rather it is about being concise.

If you normally have trouble in getting to the point during the conversation, below are the strategies which can help you curb that problem and help you improve in keeping your answers to the questions short and concise:

1. **Get ready for common interview questions**

    There are those interview questions that are commonly asked in an interview, which, when you walk into that room without preparing for them in advance, you will be a fool. For example, an interviewer may ask you to tell him/her a little bit about yourself, your background, and why you want the job. Those common interview questions, you can prepare by noting down the key points you may want to touch upon. Preparing for as many as possible will help you ease through those and preserve your brain for those questions which are tough.

2. **Take your time to reply**

There is absolutely nothing wrong with not giving responses to the questions right away. Take the time you need to deliver your reply. It is important to embrace pauses as this will help your interview feel more like a regular back-and-forth exchange and will help you feel relaxed and look more confident. You can repeat the question silently in your head and make sure you understand what is being asked. If you did not understand what is being asked, then this is the time to ask for clarification. It is also an opportunity to revisit the key points you noted.

3. **Follow a particular format for each answer**

   Having a go-to format in answering each question can be of huge help. Reply to the questions as brief as possible; for example, in one or two sentences only, following it up with background detail if necessary, emphasize the necessary and wrap it up.

4. **Recognize rambling signs**

   For you to change a certain trait, you need to know why and when it is happening. You need to find out your clues. For example, are people glazing? Are they trying to interrupt your talking? These are the signs which can help you realize you are rambling and help you to put a stop to it.

For anyone to succeed in a behavioral interview, it is all about preparing well for it. In behavioral questions, there aren't necessarily wrong responses to the questions. The interviewer is simply looking to understand you better and get to know the real you. It is very important to be open and sincere in your answers and practice to structure your replies to the questions in a way that conveys what you will bring to the position in question. The most important tool not to overlook and which you need to take time going through it over and over again is the job description. It is where you will generate all the possible questions you may be asked during the interview. Therefore, ensure that you clearly understand the details in the job description to enable you to do this. Moreover, by following the above guide on how you can prepare for your behavioral job interview, I am confident it will help you go through your interview successfully.

Chapter 4: Behavioral Interview Questions

Today, interviewers rarely ask traditional interview questions. They ask behavioral interview questions to gauge how a potential employee would behave, in particular, often challenging circumstances. These questions are based on the assumption that your past and current behavior will predict your future behavior in similar cases. They are looking for soft skills such as:

- Problem-solving, initiative, creativity
- Stress management, adaptability
- Teamwork, leadership
- Negotiation, persuasion
- Organization, planning
- Work ethic

As you prepare for the interview, ensure that you have a capsule of success stories that illustrate some of the soft skills that you employed at one time or another at your place of work in your personal life. It is essential to take these behavioral interview questions seriously and prepare adequately for them because they might help you land your dream job.

The questions below will steer you in the direction of what you should expect in a behavioral interview. The examples will help you prepare the answering strategy of every question and ace the interviewer's rating system. This rating system is merely a comparison of the consistency of your answer to a standard approved response in that given situation. Passing the behavioral interview questions complements the technical interview. These questions are often structured in an open-ended way to provide the interviewee with a chance to respond in elaborate detail.

Common Questions

Based on the skills outlined above, we shall look at some examples of common behavioral questions to expect in an interview and how to respond to them. In this book, we shall not give answer examples to all questions; however, you will receive the guidelines you need to tackle any of the other questions demonstrated here or in the interview room.

Problem-Solving, Creativity, Initiative

Hiring an experienced problem solver can be a massive benefit to a company. Interviewers seek people with high problem-solving abilities because they can manage themselves in stressful or unusual situations that demand an individual to think on their feet. Some competencies they are looking for in problem-solving skills include; creativity, initiative, drive and determination, resourcefulness, and critical as well as analytical thinking.

Q1. *Would you call yourself a functional problem solver? If so, what makes you a good problem-solver?*

Q2. *What was the most stressful situation you have ever faced at work, and how did you handle it?*

This question is testing all the facets of problem-solving. Therefore, the answer will demonstrate how you took the options available, weighed them against themselves to produce a viable outcome.

Response

Give a brief description of the situation in the workplace before you start to give an account of what made it stressful. For instance, "I once, about three years ago, worked at a wholesale company, XYZ, where my job was to sort, in order of priority, the merchandise we would be taking up for resale. The job demanded to know the products if they meet the standards approved by the state, identifying the unique quality factor in each, and if they align with the company policy."

Then describe the one time that the job got very stressful. In our instance, "One time, I had a deadline to submit a report on the next quarter of items we would be restocking. At the same time, the company was organizing a retreat where my immediate supervisor required my input to handle menial, yet urgent tasks to facilitate a smooth-running event. During this time, I found myself overwhelmed and split between two tasks that needed immediate fulfillment."

Finish off the answer with how you were able to handle the situation. "Eventually, I had to create a schedule that cycles between checking over proposals for the report and helping my supervisor with the retreat. I communicated this time-allotment to my supervisor, who commended me and abided by it. I met the reporting deadline, and we had a successful company retreat. As a token, I was granted ten paid leave days."

Q3. *Have you ever faced a situation you could not solve? How did you feel about it?*
Q4. *How do you deal with a problem you are faced with? What steps do you take to tackle it?*
Q5. *Tell us about the best idea you came up within your previous job*

How to Handle Questions on Problem-Solving?

Select an interesting example. You do not want your response to be run of the mill; you want to stand out and make an impression on the panel. Pick an example that demonstrates your outstanding abilities in the areas of analytical thinking, as well as result-oriented drive for accomplishment. Show how your approach to solving the problem sets you apart from the rest of the crowd.

In your examples, try not to generalize. Try to make the experiences as specific and detailed as possible- without losing track of the question at hand. Answers like, "Problem-solving is a big part of my day-to-day job description" are stale, and no interviewer will take you seriously after that. Specificity will help you illustrate your point further.

Remember to shed a positive light on yourself as you give these examples. You are applying for a position in their company, so you want to impress them with your skills and thought processes. Practice, practice, practice, take down a few notes to keep you on track during answering; as you take a stab at it in the mirror. Vocalize the answers and pay attention to your voice, intonation, expressions, etc.

Teamwork

Teamwork questions are essential to indicate whether an individual is capable of interacting with others in a productive way, which is necessary for almost all work environments. Interviewers, in this way, are also seeking to gauge your reactions with complicated team dynamics. Motivate, collaborate, mediate, communicate effectively, and possibly lead a team in any event when called upon.

Arrive for the interview prepared to answer some teamwork questions no matter what level of experience you may be applying for. If it is an entry-level job, the teamwork experiences will be in your personal life, for example, at school, church, social clubs, etc.

Q1. *In your opinion, are you a team player? What are your feelings about a collaborative work environment?*

Q2. *Give us examples of team projects in which you have participated.*

In this question, the interviewer is looking for information about the task that the team handled, which role you played in the organization, how you contributed to the success of the job, and how well the team interacted in the completion of said task.

Response

Discuss the project goals, and metrics, project facts, and conclusions. For example, "For two years, I worked as a quality assurance officer at a software technology company. I had to test each product for bugs, compatibility, user experience, user interface, and overall functionality before conducting what is called a 'live test' which is testing with a larger group of people in a controlled environment. After the product passed the testing phase, I would then write up a report to clear it for deployment."

"Therefore, my job required me to communicate between the testing team and the engineers. I acted as a liaison between the end-user and the engineer. Within this time, I created an online feedback channel that can be accessed by the subjects and developers alike. This platform logged all the bugs experienced by each test subject, and there was some room for comments on how the user journey could be improved. The developers, on the other hand, would access the information in real-time."

"We had twenty thousand downloads in the first week of our first application, and the download rate increased steadily by 20% over the first year. Within the two years, we deployed two fully functional applications- compatible with iOS and Android smartphones- on several online purchase sites. In two years, the company's revenue grew by a factor of 5." The outcome of every situation is the punchline to the entire question; therefore, do not neglect to mention it even if it is contextually implied.

Q3. *Tell us about a time when you disagreed with your boss or a member of your team.*

This question demands you to be completely honest, but not embarrassingly so. By this, I mean, do not give too many details about yourself and personal preferences in employee conduct. It is not uncommon to have disagreements with your colleagues, so the question is valid in any work situation to check stress management and practical communication skills.

Response

When answering this type of question, if you have not had any experience that they require you to share with them, do not embellish yours. Tell them that all your past experiences have been peaceful and productive. Otherwise, you might want to share with them something like this, "About a year ago, we had a change in office directors. The lady who stepped in charge had a different leadership strategy than the former director. She would command people in a board meeting, dismiss someone when they were in the middle of sharing a thought, or a presentation, and sometimes she would chase people out of the office past work hours to avoid paying overtime."

"In one instance, she asked me to flag down an event ten minutes before time to sweep attendants out of the venue. I respectfully called her aside and expressed my concern about mishandling our esteemed guests. I asked for a slower pace of continuance for the event to indicate winding up; instead of kicking them out. She agreed with me, and I mobilized the team to communicate with our service providers to comply with the new directive."

"We eventually got to close the event ten minutes past time, but our clients were happy with the entire event.

In the course of the next two months, we had eight clients give us their repeat business. After that day, she made sure to say hello to me every time she was at the office. Granted, she did not turn over a new leaf, but she no longer raised her voice at my team because entrusted me to them as well as the projects allocated to my department. I subdued a potentially toxic environment."

Q4. *Have you ever taken the lead in any situation at your place of work? Tell us about it.*

Q5. *How would you handle a team member who feels demotivated and therefore slacking in his/her job?*

How to Handle Questions on Teamwork?

It helps to think about the responses in advance. Reminisce about experiences you have had in the past to have a follow of events. Be prepared to share exciting challenges with a positive attitude- in retrospect (right?) Think about what excites you in a team experience to be able to keep a positive attitude and come up with suitable examples.

Tailor your responses to the job in which you are applying. Make sure to give examples closely related to the line of work you will be a part of. Consider the expertise level you are applying, the type of organization, etc. If it is a high-level management application, they would appreciate examples where you took up leadership roles and how you executed the project to success.

To further illustrate your stress management skills, the interviewers may decide to conduct a group interview. Group interviews save the interview panel many work hours. Therefore, they may ask questions to see how each of you react, whether you will boost each other's answers, step over one another (figuratively), etc. Such questions may include, "How would you describe the colleague to your left? What will you offer the company? What is unique about you?"

Organization and planning skills
If you are applying for an administration position, organization skills are required mostly in this area. The ability to allot time and energy to tasks, cohorts,

resources is necessary for almost all positions, especially in a fast-paced environment where you are required to multitask or at the very least, manage your time. Like every other skill, there is no one way to be organized; it all depends on how you stay organized. For example, a friend of mine likes first to create folders in which to direct downloaded files and then download the data directly into those folders. I, on the other hand, want to download files to the default location then sort them out later when they begin to pile up. The point here is, what works for you may not necessarily work for someone else.

Q1. *Tell us about a time when your organizational skills helped you*
Q2. *Have you ever gone the extra mile to complete a project?*
Q3. *Give us an example of how you would handle last-minute changes you would have to fit into a project you have been planning for five months*
Q4. *How do you plan for contingencies and unforeseen issues?*
Q5. *Tell us what method you use to prioritize duties in a project*

In this question, the interviewer is asking for you to describe how your organization system works in detail. Demonstrate how you can rank tasks and yet leave wiggle room to factor in contingency plans.

Response

When responding, keep in mind that time management is one of the necessary skills in any valuable employee. For example, "As a market research intern in a property management firm, my job was to scout for a potential property, we could enroll every quarter. With new acquisitions, we held a launch to inform our market and welcome our new clients. I had about one and a half months to prepare for the launch of our newly acquired clients and present my event plan to the company."

"First of all, I wrote down an action plan that I then broke down into smaller tasks that included taking pictures of the new property and getting a detailed description of it; and creating a guest list and contacting service providers, among many other tasks. I also noted the approximate amount of time it would take to complete one objective- which I factored into the deadline. I then contacted the service providers to book them for the event on the dates selected. They were the priority because I had to secure the cream of the crop and give them ample time to prepare for the event with our specifications. Then I contacted our guests to ask them to save the date."

"As I carried out the objectives, I crossed them out of my planner, one-by-one, which is another joy of completing a job. If any reasons delayed the attainment of the deadline, I would write it down and plan for it on-the-go. I managed to complete the prep for the presentation a week ahead of time. During the launch, everything fell into place, but I encountered a few mishaps but only with the rate of turn out. 80% of the guests attended the event, nonetheless."

How to Handle Questions on Organizational Skills?

Feel free to give examples of your everyday life to hammer in the point that you are well organized. Talk about how you keep a daily planner and how that helps you keep all of your appointments and plan ahead. Talk about the joy of finding order in chaos- give specific examples with each.

If possible, give facts and figures that provide credibility to your results. Also, if you are applying for a high-level position, prepare to answer questions on delegation. For example:

Q6. *Tell us about when you failed to delegate successfully*

Organizations today encourage delegation to reach customer needs more effectively. You should be able to make decisions that you will then give responsibilities to your team to carry out. Then you should be able to take accountability measures for the results of the project. As you delegate, you should be able to tell the people in your team best suited to perform specific jobs based on their strengths to maximize efficiency.

Prepare for in-depth follow-up questions to test whether you have thought through your answers; because if you were organized, you would have to have figured things all the way through.

Adaptability

Everyone handles change differently, so try to make your answers as unique as possible to have a lasting impact on the interview panel. Do you experience emotional setbacks that affect your productivity?

Q1. *What do you do to adapt to a new work environment in a unique position?*

This is a reasonably straightforward question when you think about it. We have all experienced jitters of being green, not knowing your left from your right. Here the interviewer wants to see how you handle transition because it is inevitable.

Response

"My first job was three years ago; I was fresh out of campus and had zero experience. I had applied for the position of office assistant at a printing company. At first, not only was I perplexed at the manual processes that it takes to produce a single batch of receipts, but also the jargon was a bit daunting, and I wondered if I could catch up with it all."

"Thankfully, the manual laborers in the print shop showed me the specific steps needed from start to finish; then, we had a pleasant conversation with them over lunch, where they taught me some of the technical languages."

"By the end of the first week, I had taken over the office duties seamlessly with only a few spatial reminders. The duties included communicating with our clients, scheduling deliveries, coordinating with the printers, ordering printing material, etc."

Q2. *How do setbacks emotionally affect your work?*

Q3. *How do you adapt to sudden changes in the environment, work, or natural?*

Q4. *Say you have a difficult client; how would you deal with them?*

Q5. *Tell us how you would handle service providers who fail to comply with their terms of the agreement*

How to Handle Questions on Adaptability?

We have discussed resilience as a skill in the prior categories above. However, this skill inevitably cuts across the board because change is not limited to one area. The interviewers will expect you to demonstrate flexibility and the ability to handle stressful situations because you will be immersed in an environment with new team members, new policies, and workflow.

Give thought to your answers and aim to consider all possibilities before answering. Remain open-minded because sometimes change is not planned, it just happens. Interviewers look for people with change management skills because they are more adaptable and not as easily stressed and worn out in dynamic situations.

Negotiation skills

Have you ever left the interview room beating yourself up for not standing your ground? Do you feel like you could have got a better deal? Negotiation starts at the beginning of the interview. You need to show the interview panel that you know what you are saying, therefore winning them over with your every response.

Q1. *In what area do you feel you need improvement?*

Q2. *What do you think the company needs, and are willing to bring in?*

Q3. *Are you happy with your current employer?*

Q4. *Why are you leaving your current position?*

There are many reasons to leave a position, one of them being having outgrown the role, another could be relocation, and the list goes on.

Response

"I am looking to move companies because I feel underutilized in my previous employment. I have so much more to offer than I am given a chance to. I know that I am in a position to showcase my ability with this company, given that chance."

Q5. *How much do you expect from the company? In terms of money and work privileges?*

How to Handle Negotiation Questions?

Sometimes the interview panel asks you to ask them questions. This is where you take advantage to ask questions that will make them remember you. Timing the questions is critical to what kind of answer you will receive. Also, pacing yourself while answering their questions says a lot about your confidence and composure. If they do not give you that chance to pose your queries to them, then you may opt to squeeze in your questions with your responses, or you may decide to reach out to other organizations that may have your interests at heart.

Work ethic

Q1. *Tell us about a time when you made sure that a client was satisfied with your service*

Q2. *Tell me about when you set a goal for yourself, what did you do to make sure that you met your objective?*

Q3. *What would you do if you went into a restaurant, and the service was deplorable?*

Q4. *Which is your proudest professional achievement?*

Q5. *Do you wait for someone else to correct a problem at the office, or do you have the drive to do it yourself?*

Questions about work ethic try to determine an individual's determination, and drive, accountability, respectability, and honor. Employees might have relevant experience but not enough work ethic. This skill almost guarantees the employer that their investment in you will yield completion and success in project goals.

Response

"I take the initiative to correct an error when I see one. If it is not in my department, then I take it up with the head of department or member in charge of the duty that needs alterations. I have the drive to see that the objectives of the company align with the duties of the employees to yield a favorable result."

"I have severally pitched into various departments in my previous job. I suggested a change in work schedules to cut the company budget and work hours by introducing an alternating weekend schedule with several staff members and overtime compensation. Before that, we had all the employees remain in the office for extended periods every day."

"By the end of our fiscal year, the company had cut the budget by sixty-seven percent by way of reducing overtime pay alone."

How to Handle Questions About Work Ethic?

By asking these prospective employee interview questions, you can, without much of a stretch, reveal applicants with a healthy hard-working attitude. The best applicants will have the option to give point by point, genuine instances of their recently shown tendency to work hard and go the full mile, and then some. Work ethic says that if the task is incomplete, then you will not rest until it is signed and sealed.

Chapter 5: Sample Thank-You Letters

Appreciation is a fundamental component of our day to day communication. It is whereby we recognize and are grateful to someone for something they have done for us or something that they have given us. The words "thank-you" are some of the very first few words that we learn. They are stylized "the magic words," along with "please" and "excuse me."

One may ask why you should thank someone for doing something that they are paid to do anyway, for instance, thanking a waiter for bringing your food or a gas attendant for pumping your gas. Acknowledgment and appreciation of something that has been done for us prove that we are aware of the time and effort put in by the other party in attending to us. It shows that we do not take for granted that they chose to spend the all-important resource of time with us, and not doing something else instead. It is our little way of showing that we are grateful for the opportunity cost that they undertook by choosing to be with us and forego an equally or more profitable use of their time and other resources. The same thing goes when someone gives us something for whatever reason. Thanking them for their service does not cost us anything, and it makes the service giver feel recognized and appreciated.

The Intricate Interview Process

The interview process is long and elaborate. It commences when an organization realizes the need to fill a particular position. They then create a custom-made job advertisement aiming to attract the most suitable candidates, while at the same time repelling unsuitable ones. After this, they shortlist those whose educational qualifications and professional background or experience best matches their needs. Only then do they invite the candidates for an interview.

In most cases, the interview is subdivided into several parts. These may include a written interview, an oral interview, and, in cases where the job is technical, the candidates may have to undergo a practical interview as well, to showcase their knowledge and abilities on the ground. The successful candidates are taken on by the company as new employees.

From the candidate's point of view, the interview process begins when they realize that they are ready to join the workforce actively. One then has to decide what job to look for, depending on their qualifications and skills. In today's competitive job market, this can be daunting and even frustrating. However, once a candidate has decided what exactly they want in terms of job title and responsibilities, they then scour the many online job bulletin boards and sites or engage an employment agency to look for a suitable match.

There are also some other factors to consider, including the location of the company or unit with the advertised vacancy, and what kind of benefits, if any, that the company provides for its employees. Some candidates may opt for large multinationals companies as opposed to family-owned businesses, for a variety of reasons. The next step is to wait for an interview call. This may come directly from the hiring company's Human Resource Department, or a third party if they have engaged a recruitment agency. The candidate should have done prior research on the prospective employing company.

Nevertheless, when the call comes, it is only prudent to review one's knowledge about the company, paying particular attention to the operations of the department where he/she applied. The candidate should then ensure that they are well prepared in terms of proper attire and also ensure to have enough sleep the previous night. In some companies, written and oral interviews are held on the same day.

The behavioral interview takes place as part of the oral interview. The candidate will be asked questions to judge their behavior based on previous experiences and also some hypothetical circumstances. Depending on the candidates' answers, the employer will pick the one whose aptitude and disposition fits best with their company outlook and requirements.

After the interview, the process is not yet over for the candidate. It is generally advisable to write a thank-you letter to the interviewer, appreciating the time they spent with you. In some cases, for instance, if two candidates are tied in all other aspects, a prompt, well written thank you letter may break the tie and help secure the position for the candidate.

In essence, a thank you letter should be brief and sound genuine. Thank the interviewer for their time, reiterate something that you said in the interview that you feel sets you apart from the competition, and express your willingness to learn more about the next step in the process. The letter may be handwritten, printed, or an email.

General Thank-You Letter Outline

The following is a general outline for a thank-you letter after passing a behavioral interview.

1. RE: "Thank you for your consideration"
2. Start off with a personalized greeting (such as Dear Mr. Smith," or "Hello Kenneth,") this is acceptable since you have already met the person and you have established a rapport with them

3. After the introduction, open the body section of your letter by showing your gratitude for their time as the interview was being conducted
4. Mention a specific thing that you discussed during the interview which piqued your interest. This proves to them that the letter is custom made for them.
5. Restate your interest in the job position and let them know you are looking forward to hearing about the next steps in the process
6. Let them know that they should not hesitate to contact you if any concerns or questions arise in the meantime
7. You may also include something to underline and explain why you are confident you can excel in this role.

Below are some examples of how to write different thank-you letters, depending on the target industry or company, after passing a behavioral interview.

Sample Letter 1: Formal Business Thank-You Letter

A formal thank-you letter should ideally be only one page long. It is best for a mature company with a rigid and set system. Such companies tend to value formality and stick to old tried and true processes and procedures in their operations.

Your names
Address line 1
Address line 2

Date

Interviewer's Name
Interviewer's Job Title
Company's Name
Company's Address line 1
Company's Address line 2

Dear *Mr/Ms Surname:*
RE: *Thank you for your time*
Thank you very much for the chance to interview with your company for the position of [position title] yesterday. I greatly benefited from our discussion, and also appreciate the opportunity to get additional insight into the organization. I am very interested in this position and look forward to joining your team.

Having discussed it, this opportunity feels like a very suitable match between my skills and experience and the requirements of the company. You mentioned that you need someone with strong [insert here skills], and I have extensive experience with [insert here skill or experience that is vital for the job.] In addition, I have experience in [insert here unique experience]. I have learned [insert here unique skill or combination of skills] in my current [or former] job as [current or former position] needed for your [job title] position.

Once again, thank you for considering me for this outstanding job opportunity. I am ready and willing to make any clarifications. Do not hesitate to contact me with any questions or concerns or if you need more information. I look forward to hearing from you and hope to join your team soon.

Best regards,
[Your name]
[Your address]

Sample Letter 2: Small to Medium Enterprise Thank-You Letter

Small to Medium Enterprises (SMEs) tend to be more flexible with their systems and structures so that a semi-informal thank-you letter would suffice, such as the one given below.

Your names
Address line 1
Address line 2

Date

Interviewer's Name
Interviewer's *Job Title*
Company's Name
 Company's Address line 1

Company's Address line 2
Dear *[Interviewer's First Name]*

RE: Thank you for your time

Thank you for taking the time off your busy schedule to speak with me *[yesterday]* about the *[insert Job Title]* position at *[insert Company Name]*. It was a very enlightening talk, and It was a pleasure hearing all the fine points you comprehensively shared about the requirements of this opportunity.

The information you shared about *[a particular detail about the job that you interviewed for]* sounded notably interesting.

I am confident that my particular set of skills will aid me to fit right in and succeed in this job, and it is a position that I would be eagerly looking forward to taking on.

I'm waiting to hear from you about the next steps in the process, and please feel free to contact me in the meantime if you have any questions.

Thank you again, and I do hope to hear from you before long.

Best Regards,

[Your Name]

Sample Letter 3: Start-Ups

Start-ups and tech companies are very laid back in terms of formality. They, therefore, do not mind using short, concise, casual communication. They are also very focused on technology, so writing long letters to them may even disqualify you as a contender for a job with them.

Your names
Address line 1
Address line 2

Date

Interviewer's Name
Interviewer's Job Title
Company's Name
 Company's Address line 1
Company's Address line 2
Hello *[Interviewer's Name]*

RE: Thank you for your time

I hereby take this moment to thank you for your time *[yesterday]*. I learned a lot from our conversation about [specific topic you discussed] and enjoyed the insights into the *[Job Title]* position that you expounded.

It seems like a very exciting opportunity, one that I could, I am looking forward to succeeding and excelling in! I'm looking forward to hearing updates on the same. In the meantime, do not hesitate to contact me if you have any questions or need to clarify something.

Thanks again for the great discussion.
Best Regards,
[Your Name]

Points to Note:

- Remember to send the thank-you letter soonest possible after the interview. It is best to do it within 24-hours while you are still memorable to the interviewer.

- Any of the above templates can be customized and sent as emails. That means doing away with all the address lines and using the "RE:" as the subject line.
- Double-check your spelling for handwritten letters and do a spell check with your word processor for printed letters to ensure that your message is free from errors that could cause you embarrassment or even cost you the job at the finish line!
- A handwritten letter feels more genuine, but one should be careful not to write a very long note by hand. It comes off as cluttered, and this may affect the comprehension and legibility thereof.
- Every thank-you letter to every interviewer needs to be unique and tailored specifically to the details of that particular date and interview. This means that the above are just rough guidelines, that should not be copied and pasted to every situation.
- Express sincerity by using heartfelt but professional language.

- Show attention and enthusiasm in your letter. Quote relevant parts of the discussion and show that you are eager to be part of the company, but also, be careful not to come off as too needy or desperate.
- Include something new that is not in your resume or cover letter.
- Be sure to have done your due diligence in finding out all you can about the company; before, during, and after the interview to make sure that you send the most suitable thank-you note for the company.

Having written the thank you note, you now wait for the company to get in touch as they had promised. If they do not, it is okay to call and follow up after the agreed time, but bear in mind that a lot of other things could be going on in the background, and their delay does not necessarily portend ill for you. It may take time to reach a final decision, so your check-ins should also be spaced, and not every hour or every day.

Keep up with your job search, even while awaiting a decision from a company you applied to or with which you interviewed. You might land your dream job before the others have made their decision.

Chapter 6: Expectancy of Employers and Their Tactics

An interactive interview is the best way to recognize if a candidate's appearances and behavioral traits are essential in your open business. In addition to this in a social meeting the questioner asks the candidate about an instance that happened in the past in a particular organization in which a particular behavior was showed and expected the candidate to identify a specific scenario that happened, the best way to answer this kind of question is for the candidate should not be aware of the conduct that the questioner is proving.

During a real interview, the interviewer needs to know the candidate's behavior trait and the type of job described. Sincere work makes the meeting operative and fruitful. For you to conduct an active communicative interview here are some of the tips that you need to follow:

Tips to Conduct an Effective Behavioral Interview

- You need to make a list of questions to ask every candidate when conducting the communicative interview; the questions must be both behavioral and traditional. The interactive interview queries give you the platform to compare the numerous answers and approaches that you got from other candidates. This makes the candidate selection more defendable.
- You need to find the list of the main behavioral personalities you have faith in that an applicant desires to be gifted to perform the work you are going to offer.
- Ask for the list of both communicative and outdated queries that you made of every candidate through the communicative interview.

- Plan interviews with the applicants who most seem to have the behavioral features, along with the aids, knowledge, schooling, and other aspects that you need, and you usually display for in your submission review.
- Narrow your candidate's choices based on the answers they give to the communicative and outdated interview queries
- You also need to choose your applicant with the right mix of information, involvement, and communicative traits that goes hand in hand with the job guiding your decision.
- Inscribe a job position that pronounces the behavioral traits of the candidates you need in the text. Ensure that the characteristics of the qualification segment of your work explanation list the same communicative traits.
- Identify the features and traits of the person whom you have confidence will flourish in that job. If you have the workers who perform positively in the job presently, list down the qualities, features, and services that they bring to the work which makes the job successful.

- You also need to identify and list the mandatory yields and presentation success aspects for the work opened.
- Recognize what you need the worker to be able to do in the openwork that you are going to offer. A job description and job specification are needed to define the necessities of the spot untaken.
- Note the applicants who have pleased you and caught your devotion with their credentials and experiences to supplementary shorten the list of the candidates needed in the interview. You want to plan the most competent applicants for a communicative interview.
- Assess the resumes, cover letters, and other work submission constituents you received from the candidates with the behavioral characters and features in awareness.

For a candidate to be employed by the employer in the open job advertised, the employer expects to see the following characteristics and traits when conducting a behavioral interview.

Characteristics and Traits Expected by The Employer During A Behavioral Interview

1. **Articulate**

    When you are able to express your thoughts and feelings easily and clearly in that you can speak fluently and coherently without any fear during the behavioral interview. This enables the employer to know that you will be able to express your feelings without fear of getting embarrassed anytime you see something that should not be done in the organization and when it is something recommendable you will also be happy and motivated.

2. **Accountable**

    You need to be responsible for whatever you do in the workplace, and you must give a satisfactory reason for doing it. The candidate should be able to report any incident to the employer or explain something that needs to be done in the organization.

3. **Listener**

   The candidate should be a good listener in that he or she needs to listen carefully to the questions being asked carefully during the behavioral interview and the candidate needs to answer them correctly.

4. **Perseverance**

   You should be able to persistently do something despite difficulty or delay in achieving success. You will be required to put continued effort without being tired to do or achieve something despite difficulties, failure, or opposition in a particular task once you are hired. This will make the employer know that you are persistence in any task given to be done. In other words, being self-minded.

5. **High energy**

   This is when you are active and faster at all times at work, and anytime you are given the assignment to work on, you are able to complete it at the correct time and submit it because time is of the essence, and time management is effective.

6. Confident

The candidate should be confident while answering the questions that he or she has been asked by the employer. The confidence applied will enable the employer to identify your confidence skill, and you will be good to go.

7. High integrity

You need to be highly intelligent in that you should be in a position to answer any question you have been asked by the employer during the behavioral interview. This will make the employer know that even when you are given a particular task to tackle when hired you will be in a position to do it perfectly.

8. Self-directed

This is the act of making your own decisions and organizing your own work rather than being told. It helps a lot because you can decide what is best and needed in the project or task you are told to do by the employer.

9. **Adaptable**

   You are required to adapt faster and get used to the new way of operating and doing different tasks in the new place you are hired. To adapt faster will enable you to know how a lot of things are done within a short period of time.

10. **Focused**

    The candidate should show that he or she is focused on the type of job going to be offered to him. In other words, the candidate should show hard-working skills because it is one of the skills that the employer notices first. If you are focused it will give you a high chance of being employed.

11. **Money hungry**

    This is when you really want money, trying to get money or strongly desiring money. The act of strongly desiring money in that you are actively doing your job and in a perfect way that the employer remains to admire.

12. Enthusiastic

You should be able to show intense enjoyment, interest, or approval in a project given to you by the employer once you are hired. This will show the employer that you are enjoying your job and that you are showing interest in it.

Chapter 7: Your Curriculum Vitae

Curriculum Vitae, you have probably heard of it. Heck, you have even made one. In Latin, curriculum vitae means "your life's story." Though commonly known as a resume, especially in the United States, Curriculum vitae in simple terms is a document used to highlight your work and academic history. It is aimed at showing the strong point and involvements that are most appropriate to the job one is applying for.

The Relevance of a Curriculum Vitae

Let's take a look at some of the relevance of curriculum vitae to understand more about them.

1. Your First Contact with the Employer

Curriculum vitae is the first chance you get to make a good impression on a potential employer. It's your passport to employment. How you choose to represent yourself directly determines your chances to get your dream job. Do not underestimate its significance. A good resume should present you in the best light but not over a sale. Everyone is impacted by the first impression, and sometimes these decisions can be life-changing, like choosing a new job or a life partner.

The quality of your CV makes the first impression and can determine whether or not a potential employer can consider you for an interview. The only way a hiring manager will know you have the skills they are looking for in a candidate is if they are highlighted on your resume. The demonstration is critical; for this purpose alone, it should be cautiously understood out, considered, and inscribed so that it makes an instant helpful impact on significant decision-makers. Have in mind that the individual reading it has never met you, so keep it grammatically free from error and focused, as it will be viewed as a replication of you as an individual.

2. Job Competition
Getting a job in the 21st century is not a walk in the park. The days when a high school diploma or a college degree got you, the situation is long gone.

Employers are now looking for more than just a certificate. With many tertiary institutions churning out thousands of graduates each year, one needs to stand out from the various applications sent to a company's human resource for employment. For this reason, you must have curriculum vitae that stands out. Your CV should not only detail your work history but also highlight in detail why you should be picked among the dozens of applications.

Your CV is a marketing tool for the labor market that has increasingly become more competitive. Therefore, the more you stand out, the higher your chance of securing employment.

3. Saves Time

Ever meet someone on the streets who looks worn out because of visiting different offices asking for a vacancy? A good CV will save you lots of time that you would have lost going door to door asking for employment. This document is sent in response to jobs posted by an organization or when a potential employer has requested you.

A great CV takes practice and a bit of thinking outside the box. It's about knowing what you want and how to convince your potential employer that you are worthy of the work. You need to take ownership of your curriculum vitae and understand its value so that you can come up with a quality CV. Keeping this in mind, you will save yourself lots of time.

4. It Reminds You of the Far You've Come

A good CV will remind you of how far you have come, especially when you have been successful throughout your career. This will also be a bonus if your career was shaped by working for multiple companies. However, one thing to keep in mind when applying for a job is not to have some lengthy CV. Curriculum vitae that is too long will turn off the reader, which in this case, is your potential employer. A rule of thumb is, your CV should not go back to more than 15 years; that's at least five employments or six if you go far.

You know you have worked since you were, but that won't be necessary if you have had over six employments. Keep that in mind and only include what is relevant. Besides, some jobs might not be appropriate for the present age where technology has advanced. For instance, if you repaired videotapes 15 years ago, you should not add that to your CV in a period where coding exists. That should only be for you.

5. Sell Yourself

A quality CV is not that which highlights your qualifications, but that which sells you as an individual as the ideal package. The one reading your CV should get excited just by reading it because of the qualifications and skills that you will offer the organization. The secret to doing this is to list all your background interests and abilities such as the employer sees them as possible benefits to the organization.

Instead of saying you a freelance writer, talk of what you can do for the company. For instance, I will help you write compelling and well-crafted content that will attract the reader's attention and improve your sales. Be specific; talk of how your achievements by using details.

Components of A Quality CV

A quality CV is that which has all the parts needed by the employer. You should highlight all your achievements and all the positive aspects of all the experiences you have concerning the specific job. Your CV should stand out from the rest. It should help you get that interview to the task of your dreams.

Let's look at the components of a CV to understand more about how quality should be.

1. Personal Details

A quality CV starts with a piece of personal information that should always be at the top to grab the recruiter's attention. Your profile gives an overview of who you are.

The personal details that you should include in your CV include:

- **Name**
  It might sound obvious, but people often forget that including your name on a CV is the most critical component in identifying who you are. You should write your name in a big font, bold

it and center it enough for it to stand out. Something else to remember is to avoid writing "curriculum vitae" at the top of the page as the heading.

- **Address**

The Current address is the second most vital component to include in your details. A speech in your CV is the typical writing convention, which serves as the trust factor. If you live close to the job you are applying for, your address will significantly be a benefit for you and your employer.

- **Email Address**

You should also not overlook an email address in your details. A great tip to remember is to give out your own and not your business email. The email address should also be professional, add your name and last name in it. For instance, StanSmith@gmail.com. Ensure that the email address should also be active. Not following this might break your chances of getting called for an interview.

- **Telephone Number**
    Don't forget to include your telephone number. Either your mobile number or your landline. If you are making an application to an international organization, make sure to include your country's dialing code.

There are other personal details that you might include, though not necessary. Features such as your website or LinkedIn account are essential, especially if they have additional information that can boost your chances of getting that interview call.

2. Personal Statement

A personal statement is a necessary part of your CV. It is a short paragraph, usually below your details. Unlike other components of the CV, a personal statement is typically tricky to write. Your account should contain information that includes the keywords that best describe you. The report should be brief and to the point. Words such as ambitious, motivated, trustworthy among the rest are necessary for you to get the job.

Your stamen aims to capture the attention of the employer. Remember how you write your statement depends on where you are in life. A personal account of a college leaver will be different from that of someone who has been working throughout his/her life.

A personal statement includes:

- Who you are?
- The value you can add to the organization
- What you plan on achieving: Your career aims and goals

According to an article by Forbes magazine, recruiters can tell whether a recruiter is a good fit within the first six seconds by just looking at the personal statements. Therefore, you shroud ensure the account is in line with the company's goals. Convince them that you are the right fit for the job.

Remember not to have a long paragraph. A four-sentence section is ideal. It should also be clean and concise. Ensure that it is also consistent with the rest of the CV and always in the first person.

3. Employment History

Something that employers will take a great interest in is your employment history. They do this to find out whether you have the skills and experience to work in their organization.

Always remember to be brief and show your positive nature in the job application. The following are what you should have in your employment section:

- **Name it appropriately**

    Whether you plan on naming it employment history or work experience or relevant experiences, understand the meaning behind the names first.

- **Detail You Experience Clearly**

    Experiences should be in reverse chronological order and not jumping from one decade to another. Star with your most recent employment, and be sure that this follows your education history.

- **Ensure that it is Recent**

    Though employment history is necessary, don't go listing jobs that you did decades ago. Also, ensure that the tasks are relevant to the position you are applying for in the organization.

- **Don't Describe the Job**

    Job descriptions, if necessary. Employers are not looking for what your job entailed at the previous organizations. They care about your skills, abilities, and what you have to offer.

- **Problem Solving Skills**

    The thing that employers are always looking to know is how you can deal with a problem when presented with one. Are you creative enough? Can you think outside the box? Therefore, show them how you can do it.

- **Use Numbers to Show Results**

    Employers Like to know how exactly you achieved something, and the best way to do this is through the use of numbers. So, say you boosted the company's sales by 20% instead of you boosted the company's sales.

4. **Academic Achievements**

With the high completion in job markets, you need to stand out from the rest, and a great way to do that is through academic achievements. Your academic results are just as relevant as your employment history. Be sure to include any pertinent completion like first aid because they have a significant impact on an organization.

Awards and achievement are essential; however, you should know what is necessary to add to your CV. Grants and results that provide evidence of what you have been saying in your CV. Some of the awards that you should include in your achievements are employee of the month and team player award.

5. **Your Interests**

Your interests are just as vital, so make sure you add what is relevant to the jobs you are applying for. If you participated in a charity event or worked in a voluntary sector, include it in your CV. These interests show who you are as a person that you have a caring and generous attitude. If you like spending your time with the people close to you, the recruiter will see you as someone stable and secure in your way.

6. **References**

The final part of your CV should be the references section. A two to three lists of your most recent recommendations are recommended. However, you should be careful who you add as your references and always ask for their permission. Most people usually think that it is okay to add a random person, but this is wrong. Recruiters are keen to know who they are bringing to their organization, and the best way to do it is by asking someone who knows you, in this case, your references.

Keeping in mind all the importance of CV and how it can help you get that interview, you will be kept on writing the quality Curriculum Vitae.

Chapter 8: The Team Spirit

Team spirit is a catalyst that each organization wants to accomplish for outstanding performance. Certain things will tell either if a company is sinking or it will soar, such as the strategic plans, marketing, technology, and financial investments that have been clearly shown as very vital amongst many others. A lot of productive industries will have organizational spirit or culture as their key competitive advantage. Enterprises can buy similar equipment, goods, labor, and any other tangible assets as their opponents. What is impossible for many sectors to buy is the intangible culture of caring for customers that can break all the substantial savings. For you to achieve this, then you have to be sure of reliable and robust leadership.

Many jobs cannot be done in isolation. This means that any individual from any role down there up to the managerial level should be able to collaborate in unity with other people. You should always be ready to encounter questions about teamwork when you are going for a job interview for any work. The reasonable question you will be asked about teamwork is being asked to give examples of your cooperation.

What the Interviewer Wants to Know

A hiring manager will tend to ask queries that will help them understand how you previously worked with other people in the past. This will assist the person interviewing to know-how will go along with other employees in their company. Any hiring manager will want someone who can be a team player, and this means you have to respond in a manner that shows you can work well with the other employees around.

How to Respond: "State Instances of Your Teamwork"

You should be able to enhance the STAR interview method. When you are asked to state examples of your teamwork, then you should consider this as a behavioral interview query. The hiring manager will ask you to try and reflect or think of your past experiences, and this is for you to show how you will be able to act at the new task. In any case, where you are supposed to respond to a behavioral question, the best method to use is the STAR interview answering method:

- **Situation** – You should be able to talk some context about your experience. You should the hiring manager know something a little about the team. You are allowed to give the number of people in the group, your precise role, and so on. You should not want to get into more excellent detail, but provide a little background data that is helpful.

- **Task** – You should be able to describe the team's goals and particularly the projects you were working on. In cases where your team experienced some challenges, then you should be able to talk about the problem.

- **Action** – You should describe the steps that you took to meet your teams' goals. Possibly all of you had the right attitude when it comes to delegating specific tasks and executing them. It can be possible that all of you had strong communication skills and were never involved in any conflicts by expressing your concerns quickly. This will give you an upper hand on how to solve problems effectively within your collaborative work setting.

- **The result** – You should finish by talking about the outcomes of the team's actions. You should persist on what your team was able to execute. You should be able to tell if you surpassed your goal, or the assignment you had was finished on time.

You should not concentrate so much on yourself when you are talking about the achievements that you solved as a group or what you worked for as a whole. You are demonstrating the capability you have to work with other people, and this will be with the inclusion of talking about your success with the group. Try to show that you have confidence and try to show you are positive. You should be able to express how you can work well with other people and how much you are enjoying. Thus, you are supposed to be positive in your response, and this should be seen when you are talking about your successes. In the discussion, you should not speak of anything negative concerning your team, do not point fingers at others, or complain about someone's failure.

There are qualities of a good team that can be shared at a workplace such as:

- Dedicating yourself fully to the company's mission
- You can help your team member willingly without being forced to perform a task when it's necessary
- Great inscribed and verbal communication abilities
- Better management abilities
- Strong organizational skills
- Capability to solve conflicts at workplace successfully and peacefully

At the same time, some qualities will be able to make a good team player. Such conditions that will make you a good team player will include:

- You should be committed for the team to have a successful operation with its tasks, duties, and projects
- You should be willing to assist a team member in want
- You should be committed to making sure that your team members are informed about any enhancements that are related to projects or the company's general business.
- You should be reliable, responsible, and have excellent communication abilities.

A hiring manager will only take 30 minutes or one hour to tell whether you are a qualified candidate for a position. In such cases, a lot of questions will be asked various layers, and if you don't address the sub textual queries that may not leave a strong impression. You should be able to understand different elements of questions that have been commonly used, and this can give you a great answer. You should be able to look at the explanations and sample solutions to ensure that you ace your response. You should have in mind that though there, it is right to answer the queries from the context of your existing position. You be able to respond to this, and other relevant interview queries from the perception of the job you are applying for.

Chapter 9: Dealing with Rejection after a Behavioral Job Interview

You have probably been there before, the dreaded rejection phone call, or email following a behavioral job interview. Such an experience is never easy to deal with. It is even worse if you have faced multiple rejections in the course of your job search. Such rejection can easily make you lose hope.

After every rejection, you keep asking yourself many questions; you wonder where you may have gone wrong, especially if you had prepared well for the interview. You had strong positive feelings about the whole interview experience, but when the results are out, it is far from what you had expected. You end up feeling frustrated and disheartened.

You should remember that handling a behavioral interview rejection is as important as the skills you need to secure that dream job. Allowing rejection to affect your confidence, therefore, is detrimental to how you perform in future interviews. You shouldn't allow rejection to make you doubt your qualifications and abilities.

How to Deal with Rejection After A Behavioral Job Interview

In case you receive the dreaded rejection email soon after your behavioral interview, here is what you need to remember in order to be positive, motivated, and optimistic for your future behavioral interview.

Remember it is Not All About You
It is quite easy to take all the blame after an interview rejection. You will be tempted to blame your personality on the failure to get the job. However, you should avoid making any job rejection personality issue. Job interview decisions are not based solely on your performance or the interview technique you used. There is a myriad of other factors that interviewers consider before making a decision to hire

you. So, if you had prepared well and you believe you did your best during the interview, then you should learn to relax and let it go.

Besides, most of the reasons informing hiring decisions may not be made open to you. You will be surprised to learn that you performed excellently, but other factors at play could have led to your job rejection. For example, the hiring team may have picked an internal candidate who is more familiar to their business workings, or maybe they picked someone with slightly higher experience than you.

Rejection is Never Feedback.
The greatest assumption you can make is to take a job rejection as negative feedback about you. Just because you didn't secure that job, doesn't mean everything you do henceforth is wrong. The right thing to do is to request the recruiter for detailed feedback about your interview so as to help you improve.

Alternatively, you can seek the advice of any competent HR professional in the areas you need to improve on. You will have to carry out a mock interview with the professional for you to get constructive criticism and feedback to improve on.

Don't Carry Interview Baggage Around with You

You should not carry the interview rejections of you passed to your new job interviews. Learn to approach each new job interview with a fresh perspective and a positive attitude. You should also update your CV to fit into the requirements of the unique opportunity. You should then embark on conclusive research and preparation for the new interview. Learn from the mistakes of your previous interviews and make the necessary corrections.

Every company has different hiring teams, which comes with different ideas on the ideal candidate. What the other companies failed to pick from your personality and resume may be chosen by the new hiring team, so it is therefore essential to keep a fresh approach as you get ready for your next job interview.

Keep Learning and Developing

After every rejection, it is common for your confidence to take a hit. You, therefore, need to keep your morale and motivation high after every job rejection. Endeavor to keep your skills sharpened and your experience up to date. You can do this by enrolling in a short-term training course or mentorship program. Alternatively, if you are out of employment at that particular moment, you can volunteer your skills at a relevant charity project. This will significantly aid you in boosting your confidence level. It will also enable you to focus your energy on pertinent other issues away from your job hunt. Besides, the experience will provide a discussion point in your next interview.

Learn to Stay Positive
You should always take a job rejection as a necessary step in your pursuit of success. Most successful professionals had at least faced one or more job rejections in the past. Job interview rejections are part and parcel of everyday life, and if you take them positively, then they provide an essential learning platform to make you better prepared for your next job interview. You should, therefore, embrace every job rejection positively, find out the reasons for the reaction, and focus on your next interview.

Take some moments to reflect on your past job interview and see what you could have done better. Find out what you missed and the mistakes you did, all this will inform how prepared you will be for your next interview.

Stay Connected by Sending a Thank You Letter

Most people fail to send a thank you letter to the interviewer, especially after a job interview rejection. It may appear awkward to you, but it is essential to do so. What you are trying to communicate by writing a thank you note is that you appreciate the chance you were given, and you should be reconsidered for future openings. It also demonstrates to the interviewer that you possess the necessary attitude to handle difficult or challenging tasks if given an opportunity.

Besides, the interviewees can decide to forward your details to a relevant department they feel you best fit in. They can also consider you for another role or mention you to another company that needs the skills you possess. You, therefore, need to stay connected even after a job rejection by sending a simple thank you note. Such a message can open more significant opportunities for you shortly.

Appreciate Your Effort
The moment you receive a rejection letter can be quite disheartening. You could feel so demoralized, primarily if you have attended several rounds of interviews for a particular job. However, the fact that you made it through several rounds should inform you of your high capabilities. You, therefore, need to congratulate yourself for making that far. Take a moment from your job search and go out and celebrate your achievement. Don't start searching for another job immediately. You need to wait until you are in a more positive mindset before you begin applying for fresh employment.

Ask Your Interviewer to Consider You for Future Openings
A rejection letter doesn't mean all the doors have been closed or you don't have to work for the company again in the future. You need to leave things positively for you to be reconsidered for future openings, especially if the company is one of your dream companies to work with.

Some companies keep records of all their former applicants, and they quickly pick an applicant they liked to fill in a new opening. They can also reject you for full-time positions but may consider you for contractual engagements. When you maintain a positive connection with your interviewer may result in a job down the line.

Analyze Your Resume

Whenever you receive too many rejections in a row after applying for several jobs, it is essential to take time off and analyze what could be the missing link in your CV. You might need to take a critical look at your skills and make the necessary adjustments. You need to be honest and objective to yourself so as to carry out an unbiased analysis of what the issue is. If your rejections are a result of missing skills, then you need to take the next step and enroll in short courses that will build up your skills set.

Hire a Career Coach

If you can afford to hire a career coach to help you figure out what is not working in your resumes, then that is highly advisable. Seeking professional help could go a long way in improving the missing skills and other critical considerations that led to your job rejection. A good career coach will help you figure out which skills are transferable for the target jobs. However, career coaches could be quite costly, and you, therefore, need to first reach out to your university alumni networks to access the same type of support without spending any money.

Be Flexible to the Needs of Your Next Job Search

When you finally decide to get back to your job search, you need to be more flexible when it comes to the jobs you are applying to. In case you felt uncomfortable transferring your skills or relocating to other industries in the past, then it is time to reconsider that soon after your job interview rejections. This will enable you to widen your job search horizon and increase your chances of securing a particular job.

If you are willing to be more flexible on the specific job description, then you need to widen your scope further to stand better chances of securing a job.

Take Up an Extra Project at Work to Build Your Experience and Resume

If you are employed at the moment, then it at be advisable to take another project at work to help build up your resume. This could mean adjusting your schedule and sacrificing your flexibility as you work to meet the expectations of your other projects. However, the whole experience will be worthwhile as it helps you to build up your skills that will come in handy when you seek future greener pastures.

Try Again Applying for a Vacancy at Your Dream Company

After you have built up your skills, you should take the initiative of trying out still at your dream company. If you received feedback on the hiring manager on your weak areas and you subsequently took the necessary step to bridge the gap, like going for short courses, you could always try reaching out for similar positions at the company. This will show the hiring manager you are interested in that company and that you took the rejection and subsequent feedback positively.

Apply for as Many Job Openings as Possible

You should avoid putting all your hopes on a single job opening such that when you are rejected, you become entirely crushed. In your search, you should be interacting with at least five different employers at one go. Aggressively network within those organizations to increase your prospect of getting a job. In case you are not successful at one organization, you can always focus your energy on the others. You should also replace the rejecting employer with a new promising one as soon as you get that regret letter. When you apply for a job with several companies, you can't become overly fixated on only one opportunity.

Allow Yourself Time to Grieve

You should always give yourself some time to grieve the bad news before moving on to your next job search. It is advisable to give yourself at least 24 to 48 hours to dwell on your disappointment before you rethink your future strategy. Resilient people are always successful at securing their dream job, no matter how long it takes.

Take a Walk

You can beat your disappointment and feelings of dejection soon after job rejection by taking a simple walk. Nature always has therapeutic benefits on your mood, focus, and creativity. When you are involved in any job search, make it your habit to go out for nature walks occasionally. You will gain a lot of perspective and inspiration during such simple walks. Walks will also help you deal with stress you may be experiencing soon after a Job rejection.

The Reasons for The Job Rejection

Job rejections are always unpleasant. You can get frustrated after behavioral interview rejection, especially when you know you are good at a particular job. It is, therefore, vital for you to understand what you did wrong and how to fix it. You may not get honest and useful feedback from your interviewers once they decide not to hire you. However, most job rejections happen because of one or all of the reasons below:

Failure to Keep Time

Probably you know too well you must turn up for a job interview on time, but somehow you were late for your recent interview. It doesn't matter the reason behind your lateness, turning late for an interview is always a costly mistake you should always avoid. The interviewer will get the impression that you are not serious or unreliable about the opportunity in case you are picked.

If you happen to be late, the best thing to do is to acknowledge and own up to the mistake. You can then make sincere apologies and thank the interviewer for their willingness to interview you still. For whatever reasons, don't pretend that they never noticed your lateness, they always do.

Failure to Follow Instructions

Many hiring companies ask you to come along with certain items to the interview. For example, they may require you to bring your original certificates, ID, references, or resumes. They are making these requests for a reason best known to them, and when you fail to bring them, then the impression they get is that you are weak at following instructions. Failure to follow instructions is one of the significant reasons for candidates to get rejected.

You Were Unpolished

Some specific cultural practices inform the attire of those working in a particular organization. It will be in your best interest to research the particular attire of an organization before you turn up for the interview.

Focus on the little things that can make a huge difference when it comes to your first impression skills. Avoid unkempt hair, wrinkled or stained clothing, strong body odor, or strong perfume.

You should also avoid being sloppy as this makes you look like you don't care enough to be organized and prepared. If you turn up to an interview looking unpolished, then it is an indicator to your hiring manager that they shouldn't trust you to represent the company in business events.

They Think You Won't Stay for Long with Them

When your hiring manager has doubts about whether you will last with them after securing the job, they may decide not to hire you. This could happen in scenarios where you applied for a job, which is way below your qualifications and experience. You, therefore, need to convey a clear message that you will be motivated enough to excel and last in your new role in the long term. Managers don't like hiring people who will leave after a short time. High turnover rates are quite costly to companies, and the hiring manager will do all they could to avoid such scenarios.

Awkward Nonverbal Cues
You should always strive to display appropriate non-verbal cues with your interviewer. Avoid weak handshakes, poor eye contact, and poor body posture. Your body language still conveys the loudest and strongest message to your interviewer. Practice good body posture, keep smiling whenever appropriate, and always make eye contact while speaking.

You also need to avoid awkward behavior that is socially unacceptable, for example, keeping your coat on, holding your bag on your lap, or removing your shoes during the interview.

Bonus Chapter: Tips on How to Pass the Behavioral Interview

If you are looking for a new job, then you should prioritize preparing for potential interviews. In today's job market, practicing for a traditional interview is never enough. Behavioral interviews have gained immense popularity in recent years. The top companies in the world, which you have a desire to work for, use behavioral-based interviews to hire their employees. The following are some of the tips you can use to pass a behavioral interview:

Prepare Well for Common Behavioral Interview Questions

The key to passing in any behavioral interview lies in how adequately you prepared for the interview. You need to determine which questions you will be asked to prepare the best answers. Part of your preparation also involves analyzing the job and coming up with a list of expected workplace competencies and behaviors which the company expects of its employees. The following questions will significantly help you in coming up with workplace competencies:

- What are the skills needed for the job to be done?
- What can make an employee successful in this position?
- What can make someone fail in this position?
- What are the challenging aspects of this position?

You can get a hint of what the interviewer will explore from the answers to the questions above. For example, a marketing position will most likely require excellent communication skills, adaptability, tolerance, and problem-solving skills.

You can also make use of the following tips of how to handle prepare answers touching on job-related behaviors:

I. You should focus on examples that will help you to demonstrate the expected behavior. For instance, if the behavioral question asks you to describe the time you had to go out of your way and help a client, do not bore the interviewer by giving irrelevant examples. Give relevant, clear, and suitable examples that demonstrate entirely your ability to perform the desired task.

II. Questions touching on problem-solving skills require you to come up with several courses of action once you have considered all the information and resources available for you. You then decide on the best course of action to take, and you implement it. Therefore, the behavioral answer you give must include all the mentioned critical actions so as for you to demonstrate your problem-solving ability effectively.

III. You should also avoid giving too many details as this will quickly make your interviewer lose interest in what you are saying. You need to establish the context of your story briefly but clearly.

IV. Any example that you give should center around the actions you took and how these actions contributed to the achievement of the desired goal. Avoid behavioral examples in

which you only played a minor or supporting role.
V. Come up with the right behavioral interview answers before you sit for the interview.
VI. You should also have excellent behavioral interview answers ready before the actual interview day. Take time to do a thorough review of your experience and background. Come up with good examples that highlight your strengths and skills in the given area. You should structure all your answers to behavioral questions around three components. These include the particular situation or task in which you displayed a specific behavior in question, the actions which you took, and the results of that those specific actions. This method is what is commonly referred to as a STAR. The focus of this method is for you to provide real-life examples of how you demonstrated the particular behavior or competency when subjected to a specific work-related situation.

Guidelines to Structure A Behavioral Interview

You also need to prepare and structure your behavioral interview examples to provide all the essential information required by the interviewer. Make use of the following guideline in structuring your behavioral interview examples:

1. Planning and organization

Any example you plan to present before your interview to answer behavioral questions on your ability to plan and organize should include the following actions:

- It should establish clear and realistic objectives
- It should schedule activities and time parameters that enable a job to be done
- It must set priorities
- It should state clearly the resources needed and how to make the best use for them
- It should provide a platform through which you can monitor your progress and adjustments of your activity where necessary.

2. Decision making

Any answer to behavioral questions seeking to establish how you made your judgments and arrive at decisions should include the following steps in decision making:

- Gathering of the necessary information and facts to be used in making the right decision
- Using this information to work out possible courses of action to take to solve an issue
- Taking into considerations the alternative courses of action that can be used to resolve a problem
- Taking into factors the different outcomes, implications, and consequences of various courses of action
- Carry out the most appropriate courses of action and avoiding the rest which is less relevant in solving a particular issue
- You should also state how you involve all the necessary stakeholders in your decision-making process.

3. Problem-solving

You can make use of your past examples to demonstrate how you successfully analyzed and solved a work-related problem in the past. Involve the following critical elements of problem-solving:

- Finding and gathering all the necessary information from the specific relevant sources
- Organizing and sorting the data to come up with pertinent data that will help in problem-solving
- Coming up with various possible solutions to a given problem.

4. Adaptability

Any behavioral example that you make use of to answer interview questions touching on your adaptability should contain the following elements:

- Adjustment of your behavior, communication approach, to match the changing tasks and work demands of different people within your organization and out there in the real world

- Adjustment of your priorities to meet new deadlines and information
- Adjustment of your attitude and activities to work better and effectively in a new work environment
- Willingness to try new approaches for every changed situation
- How you attempt to understand and embrace change positively.

5. Initiative

Any choice of behavioral examples you use should be able to demonstrate that you are a person who is willing to take the initiative. It should prove that you a potential employee who is:

- Ready to be proactive when faced with a situation and be ready to seek out new opportunities
- Ready to take advantage of available opportunities to come up with new ideas
- Ready to find solutions to problems even without waiting to be asked first

- Ready to come up with new strategies and apply them in existing information and knowledge
- Able to foresee the issues and challenges and come up with solutions rather than just waiting to react whenever a problem occurs
- Able to work independently and who are desiring to look for ways to continually improve themselves and their work environment.

6. Teamwork

You also need to give specific answers to behavioral questions that seek to explore your teamwork capabilities. The teamwork examples you give should show the following:

- How you exchange information freely with the rest of your team. It should demonstrate your willingness to openly offer information and ideas to the rest of the group whenever they need them

- How you are always willing to listen to and acknowledge the opinions and inputs of the other members of the team
- How you make use of empathy whenever you are dealing with the rest of the members of the team
- Whether you are willing to ask for and encourage feedback and help from the other members of your team
- How you can support team actions and decisions and prioritize the team objectives ahead of your own goals

7. Work standards

Any examples you give to demonstrate your past behavior that indicates a high work standard should have the following:

- How you set high goals and measure for your performance
- How you impose standards of excellence on yourself
- If you are not satisfied with average performance

- Whether you are willing to assume responsibility and accountability for your successful performance and failures

8. Communication

Your answers to behavioral interview questions focusing on your communication skills should demonstrate the following:

- Your ability to listen with empathy and respect
- If you can listen attentively without interrupting whenever others are speaking
- How you receive the right message by asking appropriate questions and seeking clarifications to answers, you didn't grasp well
- How you express yourself effectively and clearly to be understood by others
- How you use appropriate language and communication styles to match the person you are communicating with.

9. Creativity

You also need to prepare examples for behavioral interview questions that seek to determine your creativity. If you are a creative person, then you should be willing to generate new ideas. You should also demonstrate your ability to approach tasks and processes differently to come up with non-traditional solutions to give problems.

Creativity is one of the most valued and sought-after qualities by employers. This is because today's workplace needs creativity for companies to stay competitive and successful.

Include Enough Details in Your Answer

Whenever you are answering behavioral interview questions, you should be detailed and specific. The examples which you use to answer the questions must be detailed and relevant to the question being asked. Avoid giving out irrelevant details. Learn to stick to the facts and clearly outline in great detail the actions you took to arrive at a desired goal or objective.

Listen Carefully to Each Question Asked

One of the critical factors that may contribute to your success in an interview is your listening skills. You need to pay great attention to what the interviewer is asking. Make sure you can understand the question well before giving out your answer. In case you are not sure what the interviews are looking for from a particular behavioral issue, then seek for clarification. For example," Are you asking me to describe a specific situation where...?" Seeking clarification whenever you have doubts about the requirements of a question will also give you time to think about your answer. You can also take a little time to formulate your response to the questions asked.

Use Recent Examples in Your Answer

You should give details of your most recent behavioral stories whenever you are answering behavioral interview questions. This is because such information seems much easier for you to recall and therefore narrate easily. Your interviewer will also find new information to be much more relevant and valid.

In case your work experience is limited, don't fear to make use of the skills you gained from your internships, college, or school you can also make use of your past projects, participation in sports, community service or even your hobbies and interests which are relevant to the job at hand.

Ensure the example you are giving out demonstrate the behavior that is being explored. For instance, in case you are asked about how you handle a conflict in the past, you can pick an example from your own family life to demonstrate that you are good at conflict resolutions.

Handle Negative Situations Confidently

Some of the behavioral questions you may be asked will seek to find out how you responded to particular negative circumstances in the past. For example, you may be asked," tell me about a specific time in the past when you were unable to solve a problem and what you did about it."

To adequately answer such a question, you will need to prepare relevant examples of negative experiences. Make use of the ones you were able to get something positive out of and which it offered you some valuable lessons.

Vary Your Examples

You need to avoid giving out the same examples for different behavioral questions you are being asked. Be creative enough and vary your response. Think of various situations from the different areas of your career and life. Go through your resume again to get fresh ideas that may help you to come up with relevant, unique responses. You should also strive to give examples that have a beginning, middle, and conclusion. You should also provide all the details on the situation, the actions you took, and the outcome from those actions.

Stick to the Facts

This is one of the most important contributing factors to passing behavioral interviews. You need to give honest and candid answers at all times. When you exaggerate your responses, your interviewer will find out by subjecting you to further questioning.

Stick to specific details of the story you are giving whenever you are answering behavioral interview questions. In case there is no specific example to relate with, you can provide a hypothetical situation. You should also avoid generalizing several related events whenever you are answering behavioral questions.

Be Aware of Your Body Language

Body language is key to passing a behavioral interview. You may be communicating using the spoken word, but your body language will be giving out the most influential and loudest message. You should, therefore, make sure your body language is congruent with your verbal communication signals. Whenever you send a positive message, and you reinforce it with appropriate non-verbal cues, your responses will appear more convincing to the interviewer.

Practice Your Answers

If possible, ensure you rehearse your answers aloud well before the interview day. You can roleplay the expected interview questions with a friend. You also need to practice the answers to the questions when you are roleplaying. If you don't have anyone close to roleplay with, you can take a video of yourself and ask for feedback from a relevant person or HR professional. The more you practice your answers, the more confident and comfortable you will be during the actual interview.

Come Up With a List of Competencies, Attributes, and Skills

The best thing about behavioral interview questions is that you get an opportunity to demonstrate your talent, ability, and results. To pass in the interview, you will need to come up with particular competencies, attributes, and skills the company is looking for. Most companies seek similar attributes, such as your ability to focus, meeting deadlines, attention to detail, etc. You, therefore, need to research these attributes and take a moment to come up with a clear list that will address the expectations of the job you are applying to.

Create a List of Your Experience

You also need to come up with a clear list of your past experiences, which may be relevant to the behavioral interview you are attending. You should also include all the successes that demonstrate your competency level. Besides, list down all the skills and attributes that played a role in the ultimate successes which you mentioned. You can also come up with good exciting stories that are detailed and are relevant to the job you are being interviewed. Take great care to keep your answers focused, brief, and consistent.

Focus on the Good and the Bad
You need to vary the examples you are giving when answering behavioral questions. Come up with situations that proved more challenging to handle. Demonstrate what you did in such scenarios to successfully arrive at the desired outcome. Your interviewer will get to understand your problem-solving skills from such examples. You will also be demonstrating your ability to handle challenges professionally in the future in case you are faced with one. Your interviewer may also ask you how you will handle such situations differently in the future and so you might need to prepare how you will discuss your areas of improvement during the interview.

Make Use of the STAR Method
When you are coming up with specific examples, you need to present it in the STAR method. This means you need to write down the particular situation or task you had to resolve, the actions you took, and the

results from those actions. You also need to make use of specifics, for example, the people involved, the places of action, the scale and scope of the problem, actions, and outcomes. All the details you provide must be verifiable in case the employer decides to do a check.

Take a Look at Your Past Performance Documents and Appraisals

To prepare well and pass in behavioral interviews, you need to take a moment and look back at your previous performance appraisal. Such an evaluation will help you to identify specific achievements and situations that will help you to come up with examples and answers for behavioral interview questions.

Start Your Preparation Now

In case you are currently working, and you want to pass in future behavioral interviews, then you need to start your preparation as early as now. You can start by documenting all your successes and achievements at your current workplace and in your past. When you document your current activities, it will significantly help you to come up with stories and examples of behavioral interviews you may attend in the future. It will also come in handy when you are completing your performance appraisal whenever you are asked to do so.

What Does the Interviewer Want in Behavioral Interview Answers?

What the interviews want in behavioral interview questions is your actual example from your experience, which is relevant to the job you are being interviewed for. What they don't want in answers to behavioral interviews are the following:

Giving out vague general responses - You need to avoid giving out generalized solutions that are not specific to the expectations of the questions you were asked. You, therefore, need to avoid using such phrases as "... most of the time.... usually" whenever you are answering your interview questions.

Making opinions rather than answering questions - You need to avoid giving your own views to the questions the interviewer is asking you. The interviewer is not interested in your personal opinions. They are looking for real-life and factual examples that you used in the past situation and which demonstrate your ability to handle a specific task at hand.

Theoretical answers - You need to avoid solutions that tell what you would do if faced by a particular situation. Give answers that indicate what you did to solve a specific issue. You, therefore, need to avoid such phrases as ".... if a had.... I would have. I might."

Common Mistakes to Avoid Doing Behavioral Interviews

While it is difficult to determine the outcome of an interview, you need to try to learn how you could increase your chances of being hired by avoiding some common mistakes. These mistakes could contribute significantly to your failure. Here are the most common behavioral interview mistakes and what you should do to prevent them:

Failing to Prepare

You need to approach a behavioral job interview in an exact manner you would an exam. You must do thorough research to get detailed information about the company you are applying to. Determine the skills that the company requires and whether your skills set can match the job expectations.

To have an edge from the rest of the applicants, research on all the recent going ins of the company, such as if the company carried out any recent mergers or if they adopted the new business model. Doing so will demonstrate to the hiring manager that you have a strong passion for the specific role they are interviewing you for.

Failing to Research Your Interviewer

You need to go to the interview with all the information about the person you will be conversing with. When you carry out such research, you may end up discovering a shared interest that you can talk about to build up a rapport with your interviewer. You may also find out that your interviewer has secure connections with one of your past employers.

Putting on the Wrong Outfit

First impressions matter when it comes to the behavioral job. When you show up at your interview while looking too informal or disheveled will communicate the message that you are not serious even before you introduce yourself to the interviewers.

Not Being Punctual

You need to arrive at the interview venue a few minutes early. Experts recommend that you arrive at least 10 minutes before time. When you come way ahead of expected time, it proves to your interviewer that you are organized, reliable, and eager. You will also get the much need time to compose yourself and familiarize yourself with the interview environment. You also get time to make use of the restroom and prepare well for the interview conversation.

However, don't be tempted to arrive too early. Doing so may only serve to inconvenience your interviewer. It also irritates your interviewer as you appear too desperate and thus can set off the interview on a wrong footing. In case you arrive too early, it inadvisable to sit in your car until when 10 minutes are remaining before the interview commences.

Using Your Cellphone During the Interview

If you keep stealing glances at your cellphone during the interview process, you will appear rude and inattentive. Avoid using your phone even if you are checking the time. It could also suggest to your interview that you quickly get distracted.

It is therefore advisable to keep your phone off before you enter the interview room. Turn off all the devices and store them out of sight until the interview is over. In case you are used to using your devices to take notes, in an interview scenario, make use of a pen and a paper and carry a real calculator along just in case you need to make some calculations.

Asking Questions with Obvious Answers

You should avoid asking questions that will betray your ignorance of the company's basic information, which are readily available with simple research. If the information can be found on the company's website, then it is your job to know about it well in advance.

There is no excuse you can give for failing to do little researches on the company you applied for. When you fail to carry out the necessary research, you will appear as a candidate who is only interested in the job and who doesn't care much about the employer.

Talking Bad About Past Employers

When you dwell excessively in criticizing your former employers, you come out as a person with an appalling attitude. The interviewer will probably conclude that you will talk about them and their company in the same way you describe your former or current employers. It doesn't matter the experience you had with your former employer, focus on their strengths, and ultimately leave their weaknesses during interviews.

Getting Too Personal

It is okay for you to use a friendly tone when you are carrying out a conversation with your interviewer. However, you should be careful not to cross the line by sharing too many personal details, which could not only be irrelevant to the job you are being interviewed for but could also make your interviewer quite uncomfortable. You never know how your interviewer will react to your personal stories. Besides, you only have minimal time with the interviewer, and it is best to make every second count by narrating your past experiences, which could help you secure the job. Therefore, you need to stay focused on all your professional accomplishments and the company's needs.

Asking for Salary and Benefits Details Too Soon

It is advisable not to bring up the issues of salary first because it will put you in a weaker negotiation position. Besides, when you talk about salary too soon after settling for an interview, you create an impression that all you care about is what the job has to offer in terms of perks and benefits. You need to postpone any salary negotiation until when you have been offered the job.

Failure to Anticipate Questions About Salary

You need to be well prepared to answer your employer's questions regarding your expected salary. Do a simple research on what the company pays for the position you are applying for. You should then quote slightly above what the company offers at the moment. You should also be ready to give justifications to your expected salary.

Moreover, don't quote too low or too high. Quoting too little will give the impression that you are not sincere or you are desperate. When you quote too high, you will appear unrealistic.

Having Poor Body Language
You need to employ appropriate body language to reinforce your verbal messages during your interviews. You should now that communication goes beyond the spoken word; it is therefore essential for you to make appropriate eye contact whenever you are conversing with your interview. You also need to offer a firm handshake that communicates the message of confidence. When sitting, use appropriate sitting posture and make use of proper public space. Do not show any signs of nervousness by fidgeting, avoiding eye contact.

Lying

This is one of the costliest mistakes to engage in during your behavioral interview. When you lie, your interviewer will know, and you will lose your chances. Besides, in case you survive through the interview, the company may discover the truth in the future, and you will most certainly be fired and legal measures instigated against you. It pays to be honest, remembers it is not a must for you to have ready answers for all the questions. If you face any challenge coming up with a solution for a particular question, admit that you don't know, but you are willing to learn.

Failing to Sell Your Skills

You shouldn't assume that your interviewer will remember all the details you wrote in your resume. You need to talk about your past achievements, the awards you have won, and the sales you have exceeded in your past or current employment. Learn to take credit for all your achievements and explain clearly your qualifications and talents, which are relevant to the job you are being interviewed for.

Selling Yourself Too Aggressively
On the other hand, you should avoid selling your skills and capabilities too aggressively to your interviewer. Avoid bragging about your achievements as this will give the impression that you are arrogant. You should also avoid dominating the interview conversation. Don't be tempted to take over the interview conversation or control the situation too much. You only succeed in coming across as an overconfident controlling freak.

Neglecting to Ask Questions
Probably at the end of every interview, the interviewer will ask you if you have any questions for them. If you fail to take advantage of this opportunity, then you will make a costly mistake. It sends the message that you are not interested in the company, or you arrogantly assume you know everything about the company.

You need to keep asking relevant questions throughout the interview so as to generate an organic, flowing conversation. This will give the interviewer the impression that you have a lot of interest in the vacant position and the company.

Faking the Answers to Questions About Your Most Significant Weaknesses

When the interviewer asks about your biggest weakness, it is easy to be tempted to give an acute response. This will, however, indicate that you lack self-awareness and that you can't handle constructive criticism or that you are not taking the interview seriously.

Conclusion

Thank you for making it through to the end of *Behavioral Interview: Pass More Easily A Behavioral Interview Because You Are Totally Relaxed. Relax Your Mind and Learn to Believe in Yourself*. Let us hope that it was informational and able to provide you with all the tools you need to get relaxed and successful in a behavioral interview. By finishing this book, you will be able to possess the mastery that you seek in enhancing your chances of winning employment opportunities.

We have gone through the understanding of behavioral interview and its key concepts. This book has offered easy-to-use but very powerful and effective tools and techniques that can help you get acquainted with behavioral interviews and how to feel relaxed during an interview. You are now familiar with the common questions that employers ask during a behavioral interview, and the ways you can respond to them to increase your chances of being successful in every behavioral interview. You have also learned about how to draft thank you letters, in which you understand how to write to your future employers, thanking them for giving you an opportunity to be part of their team.

For this book to work for you, it is vital that you encompass all the advice and techniques you have read herein. It may not be in the order that I listed them in this book, but you must use all of them for maximum benefits. You are now aware of the steps you need to take to start appreciating your empathic nature as well as empaths around you. The next thing you would want to do is put in a request for what you want. Believe in what you want and have settled on is important, and you should not allow any doubts to creep in after.

Finally, if you found this book useful in any way, a review on Amazon is always appreciated!

www.ingramcontent.com/pod-product-compliance
Lightning Source LLC
Chambersburg PA
CBHW030943240526
45463CB00016B/1546